AMERICAN
PRESIDENTS
A DARK HISTORY

AMERICAN PRESIDENTS
A DARK HISTORY

MICHAEL KERRIGAN

METRO BOOKS
NEW YORK

Metro Books
122 Fifth Avenue
New York, NY 10011

Editorial and design by
Amber Books Ltd

Project Editor: Sarah Uttridge
Designer: Jerry Williams
Picture Research: Terry Forshaw

ISBN: 978-1-4351-2695-4

Printed and bound in China

1 3 5 7 9 10 8 6 4 2

CONTENTS

PROLOGUE

New York City sweltered in the heat of summer on 1 July 1893. Those at work in factories, shops and offices sweated and complained. The rich and powerful had bolted for their coastal playgrounds some time since. Important affairs of state had kept President Grover Cleveland on duty till the

end of June, but now at last he was heading north to Massachusetts. He was doing so in some style, however: his good friend Commodore Elias C. Benedict had lent him his yacht, the *Oneida*, for the voyage to Buzzard's Bay.

Dazzling sunshine lit up the lapping waters of Long Island Sound; a brisk breeze brought welcome freshness; it was the perfect weather for a coastal cruise. Chuffing steadily eastward, the 75-ton steam yacht was taking full advantage of the calm conditions. There would be choppier waters to come, when the *Oneida*

The whiter-than-white house. With its gracious poise and its Palladian symmetries, 1600 Pennslvania Avenue proclaims the purity of American ideals – but there have been darker goings-on behind these dazzling walls.

emerged into the open Atlantic and swung round to the north. In the shelter of the Sound, though, the sea was like a lake.

An idyllic picture of affluent America at play? That was the idea, and there's no doubt it was convincing. In busy times of turmoil, Cleveland was taking a well-earned rest. The press reports of the President's vacation gave an impression of calm and confidence: Cleveland and his administration had everything under control.

A more curious reporter might have wondered why the President was taking his Secretary of War, Daniel S. Lamont, on this pleasure trip, but then care was taken that this detail did not get out. He would have been still more intrigued to learn that those on board the *Oneida* included an array of eminent surgeons, doctors and dentists, but the President's guest list was kept strictly under wraps. What sort of 'vacation cruise' begins with large and unwieldy gas tanks and strange technological paraphernalia being taken on board ship? Fortunately, it was all smuggled on in the utmost secrecy, so no one asked. Benedict's yacht had even been entirely repainted in a different colour in readiness for the 'cruise', to throw even greater

> For the President and his staff, the operation had been a complete success – though as far as they were concerned it had been a PR rather than a medical operation.

confusion over what was going on.

Scarcely had the *Oneida* weighed anchor, though, than the medical team got busy. Cleveland was strapped into a chair, secured to the vessel's mainmast for stability. A skilled dentist having administered nitrous oxide and ether, Cleveland was away in moments, and surgeon Joseph Bryant was prising open the President's mouth to reach his jaw. The suspected tumour which had caused Cleveland's physicians so much concern turned out on probing to be far larger than anticipated, but Bryant was bold and decisive: he ended up removing much of his patient's hard palate and upper jaw. In a follow-up operation, an orthodontist fitted rubber replacements which worked so well that the President's speech was if anything clearer than before.

Reporters *did* wonder why the President was so reluctant to talk immediately on his disembarkation at Buzzard's Bay. But they bought the official insistence that he'd had a toothache treated. For the President and his staff, the operation had been a complete success – though as far as they were concerned it had been a PR rather than a medical operation. The US President is two things – a man (no doubt in time a woman) and an emblem, an institution. The first has frailties, physical and moral, the other not. Covering up the discrepancy between the two has been a large part of the business of the Presidency since the office was created two and a quarter centuries ago.

INTRODUCTION: AN OFFICE IS BORN

No office on earth brings with it greater influence than the US Presidency does, but with unimaginable power comes unthinkable responsibility. Understandably enough, many holders have felt themselves to be all but crushed beneath the weight of their country's idealistic expectations.

'Americans ... still believe in an America where anything's possible.'

America was an ideal before it was ever an actual nation: the Founding Fathers had a vision and made it real. They looked across the Atlantic to an Old World in which power was chronically corrupt, from the courts of kings to the palaces of the Papacy. It should have been so different, of course. Philosophers like France's René Descartes and scientists like Sir Isaac Newton in England had ushered in an Age of Enlightenment. Their insights had helped clear the way to a new understanding of

England's 'Merry Monarch', Charles II, meets the notorious Nell Gwynn, his orange-seller mistress. America's Puritan founders despised the open decadence of the Old World societies they had left behind.

the universe. There was no need for people to be kept down in ignorance or chained in poverty any longer: humankind had a very special destiny.

Knowledge, the Enlightenment thinkers saw, could set men and women free. Reason could come to the rescue of the oppressed. Far from being blind to these new developments, Europe's tyrannical rulers saw and understood them all too well. They had no interest in giving up their privileges and power. Neither did a Catholic Church whose leaders were hand-in-glove with Europe's kings. They did their best to suppress the new learning and the spirit of liberty that went with it. And overall, it has to be admitted that they didn't do badly: the mass of people were lost in suppression and sunk in superstition.

Fathers and Faith

Men like Benjamin Franklin, Thomas Jefferson, John Adams and Alexander Hamilton were thinkers first and Founding Fathers only second. Their ambition in establishing the United States wasn't to set themselves up at the head of a new nation but to break what was becoming an intolerable British hold on their country and to realize the reign of Enlightenment on earth. For the most part they distrusted religion – or at least any role it might assume in the running of the state. Looking to Europe, they saw a collaborationist Catholic Church whose cardinals cavorted with mistresses, while their priests bamboozled the peasantry with Latin, justifying their poverty and oppression. So even the believers among them were eager to sign up to the famous secularism of America's Constitution: no one, however virtuous, would dictate to others what they should believe.

Yet it wasn't quite so simple. The New Republic may have been an avowedly secular state, but at the popular level it had (then as now) a religious streak a mile wide. Many of the first settlers had, of course, been Puritans, devout Protestants fleeing persecution by the authorities of the Anglican Church in England and by established churches elsewhere in Europe. For them, the New World represented a safe sanctuary for their Protestant observances and they quite naturally saw their lives here not just as an emigration but as a spiritual rebirth. And, though many of America's leading intellectuals did regard themselves as free-thinkers, who'd left their inherited Christian beliefs behind, they were more concerned with upholding religious *freedom* than with stamping out religion. They were secularists because they didn't want one dominant church or movement trampling another's rights rather than because they wanted to abolish religion altogether.

All Eyes on America

Not that there was any great likelihood of this ever happening. America feared God more than it feared its Founding Fathers. 'No Taxation Without Representation' may have been the colonists' call to arms when the crunch with England came, but religious resentments had been bubbling under for generations. If America felt it was a place apart, it wasn't because the Atlantic Ocean separated them so emphatically from the Old World in geographical terms but because its people felt they were striking out in a new direction morally and

Even allowing for the exaggerations of the Protestant propagandists, the Papacy was undoubtedly corrupt. The excesses of Pope Alexander VI made a mockery of his supposed status as successor to St Peter.

GOV. JOHN WINTHROP.

spiritually. They were engaged, they strongly believed, in building a new society that wasn't going to be sinful like the old. That's not to say that there weren't no-goods and ne'er-do-wells among the colonists, of course: man for man (and woman for woman) they probably weren't any better than anyone else. The feeling was strong that they *should* be, though, and whatever weaknesses this or that individual might have,

Their ambition in establishing the United States wasn't to set themselves up at the head of a new nation but to break what was becoming an intolerable British hold on their country.

John Winthrop's vision of the 'City on a Hill' has inspired generations of Americans in the centuries since, including many millions who never knew the preacher's name or shared his religious creed.

they shared a strongly rooted moral purpose. America wasn't going to be a nation like all the rest, its people told themselves: it had a special responsibility to show the way.

It had been the Protestant preacher John Winthrop who'd first voiced the idea of the 'City on a Hill'. The phrase came originally from Christ's Sermon on the Mount (Matthew 5, 13–16), of course. Jesus warned his followers that the whole world would be watching the way they lived. The City on a Hill stands out in pride, he pointed out – but potentially also in disgrace; its actions can't be hidden from the world at large. It's an example to everyone, its deeds – and misdeeds – promptly judged. In all probability, the

Founding Fathers never even knew Winthrop had existed: his works weren't widely circulated till well on in the nineteenth century. What's striking to us today is not so much that they signed up to Winthrop's Christian beliefs – because they clearly didn't – as that they shared his intense self-consciousness, his feeling that he and his little community were on display. The Founding Fathers too felt that their great project was

> Moral perfection is hard for humans to achieve. Yet the United States has always felt at some level that this is what's required; that its leaders should stand out as exemplars.

exposing America to the unsparing judgement of outsiders; that they had to be seen to be better than those from whom they were breaking free.

That sense has never left America in the centuries since, and though Winthrop's phrase has become a cliché, it's never quite lost its power to stir the spirit. Yet if it's been a source of enormous patriotic pride, it's also been a constant cause of anxiety and shame, because moral perfection is hard for humans to achieve. Yet the United States has always felt at some level that this is what's required; that its leaders should stand out as exemplars.

A Question of Standards

It's important to remember just how unusual this is. In most times and places, people have viewed their leaders more sceptically – and more tolerantly. The view that every French politician of any importance will have at least one mistress may be a stereotype, but history tells us that it's frequently been true. And there have been many countries in which financial corruption has been endemic; within reason, indeed, it's been accepted as OK.

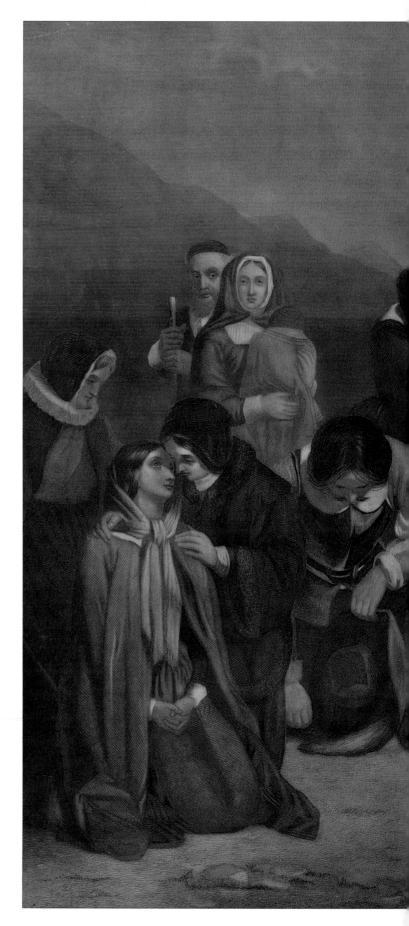

The Pilgrim Fathers came with an explicitly religious, ambitious and clear intent to build a brand new and moral society, in direct contrast with the corrupt one that they had left behind in Europe.

The Roman Empire didn't for the most part hold itself up as a beacon of morality – except in so far as might was right. And whilst the decadence of the Imperial court was nothing less than legendary, the legions upheld the military virtues to the very end. The same went for the kings of medieval and early-modern

Thanks to its infamous orgies, imperial Rome has become a byword for decadence and degeneracy: writers like Juvenal and Seneca were scathing about their rulers' conspicuous consumption and moral laxness.

Europe: bad behaviour was more or less expected; what mattered was the authority of their rule. No one really minded that Britain's Charles II had so many mistresses: the antics of the 'Merry Monarch' merely drew a smile. As for the Rome of the Popes – well, for sure, the successor of St Peter was supposed to set high standards, but this was a 'fallen' world, with everything that implied. Ever since Eve and Adam ate the fatal fruit, mortal men and women had been but sinners. They should strive, but we had to forgive them when they failed.

Does it make America 'better' that it expects much more of its politicians? That's actually very difficult to say. Do we judge by our moral aspirations (the standards that we set) or rather by the reality (the fact that so many fail to meet them)? Yet, easy as it is to sneer at the hypocrisy that so regularly seems so deeply embedded in the American Way, would it really be better to accept an ethical free-for-all?

It's got to be a good thing – surely – that we expect our representatives not to sell their influence to the

A PROBLEMATIC PROPHET

JOHN WINTHROP MAY HAVE ARTICULATED the spirit of the American Republic better than anyone else, but – his historic soundbite apart – he has his limitations as a role model. For one thing, his deeply felt egalitarianism puts him at odds with the 'American Dream'. Those of his flock who flourished, he always argued, had a responsibility to see to the well-being of their fellows before they thought about building better homes or living more affluently. The community had to come before the individual, in other words: to many Americans today, this would smack of socialism. But he believed every bit as passionately that differences of rank should be preserved: the aristocracy were born to lead, he argued. He claimed divine backing for his view: kings reigned by right in the Old Testament, he pointed out, and – since Kings and Queens were symbolic parents – any sort of popular power was in clear breach of the Commandment 'Honour thy father and thy mother'. Just in case this left any ambiguity, Winthrop went on to spell his objections out: 'Democracy is ... the meanest and worst of all forms of government.'

highest bidder or enrich themselves at our expense. Even if then they go ahead and do it anyway ...

All the President's Powers

The powers of the Presidency are immense: and always were, even at the outset when the United States were just a bunch of upstart colonies. Though he himself was democratically elected, the President was accorded enormous authority by the Constitution of 1787, which gave him an effective right of veto over measures passed by the legislature. In principle (and frequently in practice) that means one elected official squashing laws agreed by other elected officials, but then democratic government has always been about the art of compromise. The

> Even in American political discourse we talk in principle of the separation between the 'man' and the 'office', but it's harder to maintain this separation in fact.

President gets to appoint key members of the judiciary and, though in theory always accountable, has sweeping powers to overrule state legislatures. He can also withhold information from Congress when (in his view) there are grounds of national security. Whilst in theory the right to declare war is reserved to the elected legislature, the United States has actually declared war only five times in its entire history (that's right, five). Effectively, the President has the right to send US troops wherever he feels they're needed: Presidents have acted without congressional say-so over 120 times. There's no doubt that, with the powers invested in him, the US President is in a position to a great deal of good – and conversely, of course, a great deal of harm.

The moral responsibilities of a US President are commensurately awesome: in some ways that might be seen as an unfair burden. Even in American political discourse we talk in principle of the separation between the 'man' and the 'office', but it's harder to maintain this separation in fact. A corrupt cardinal wore his scarlet robes when serving in his official capacity as prelate; he took them off (one assumes) when tumbling with his mistress. A European king's authority was unquestioned, but it was vested clearly in his crown and sceptre: when he put those aside, he was just another man – albeit a very rich and privileged one. But when we look at Barack Obama – just as when we looked at George Washington – the man and the statesman are very recognizably the same guy.

And so it's always been. It's perhaps an impossible tightrope that the President has to walk: to be extraordinary and ordinary at the same time. The photos in this book underline it: US Presidents don't wear ceremonial robes (unless they're being awarded honorary degrees by universities or colleges). They

The war that never was: the United States never officially acknowledged its hostilities in Vietnam, though it might surprise the thousands of American (and Vietnamese) families who were bereaved to know that.

DON'T SWEAT THE SEX?

SHOULD WE WORRY ABOUT sex scandals at all? We elect our representatives to govern the country, not their carnal wants. Their obligation to us is to discharge their public duties conscientiously and effectively: their duties to their spouses and families aren't our concern. In some European countries, that's the generally held assumption – and some would say that Americans should take a more 'sophisticated' line. Who are we to judge? Most of us don't face their temptations – and when we do, of course, a great many of us succumb.

Yet there are arguments the other way: many people take exception to offences of this sort for religious reasons, but there are more pragmatic grounds for feeling unease as well. Can we really compartmentalize the private and the public so completely? When, in order to get what we want, we're capable of lying deliberately and systematically to our family, are we fit to look after the public finances and the legal system? What if we find there's something else we want and that we can get only by lying? The record's shown that they may well be ready to stretch a point. Of course, the European model operates on what Bill Clinton would call a 'don't ask, don't tell' assumption: the political partner knows well what he or she is getting into to begin with, or so it's said. Fine, if they've really made that choice, but even so a great many Americans will look askance at what is self-evidently a sort of institutionalized hypocrisy.

Left: Barack Obama, seen here with wife Michelle, was swept to the White House on a tide of idealism and optimism. He was elected at the end of 2008 but was it only a matter of time before cynicism as usual was restored?

Above: The son of former President George H.W. Bush, George W. Bush was widely dismissed as a lightweight and a clown. Smart enough to know his limitations, though, he surrounded himself with his father's old advisers.

stand before us as men – important men, certainly – in frock coats and business suits, like so many millions of middle-class Americans of their age. Often they pose with their 'First Ladies', looking like the other hostesses of their time, elegantly turned-out, to be sure, but clearly 'of this world'. Britain's recent elections have brought talk of an 'Americanized' style of politics in which party leaders have been put forward in a 'Presidential' manner: one key ingredient has been a frenzied media 'war of the wives'. US Presidential TV debates often dwell disproportionately (to European eyes) on a competitive assertion of family-feeling on the candidates' part.

A regular guy who likes a beer and a Commander-in-Chief with his finger on the nuclear trigger; a man who can talk baseball and trade treaties with equal ease; a man (or soon, perhaps, a woman) who must

be seen to put country above all else, yet who has to be seen to put family above all else as well.

Cronies and Corruption
One other tradition which sets the US system apart from that of many other democracies is the extent of the President's freedom to make personal appointments to his administration. Work which in other countries would fall to elected officials or career civil servants, long-time professionals, is given instead to the trusted friends and advisers of the President. There are advantages – and opportunities for abuse.

Civil servants become set in their ways; they have an overpowering instinct to stick to the tried and tested, when what Presidents want – what electors have often voted for – is change. At the same time, though, they have a long training for what they do;

Lobbyists perform an important role in bringing the concerns of special interest groups to government. The potential for abuse is always there, however, with the danger that democracy becomes the plaything of big business.

they have clear hierarchies which help ensure that their work and the decisions they make are strictly overseen. They also have a loyalty to the state as a whole, which goes beyond the obligation they may feel they owe to the man who for the moment is their chief. Practically every Presidential candidate trumpets his claims to be an 'outsider' in the alien world of Washington DC, but there's no doubt that the nation's capital can be a strange and forbidding place. Yet, whilst it's natural for the man in what can be the loneliest job in the world to want to surround himself with people he knows he can rely on, too often they know they can rely on him

for favours. Over time, it's very clear, cronyism has been one of the besetting sins of the US Presidency.

Buying a Voice

The rise of the professional lobbyist has been one of the more depressing trends in modern American political life, though its founding principle could hardly be more democratic. Every American has the right to take his or her concerns to the government in Washington. You wouldn't want it any other way. The first organized groups of lobbyists got under way during the railroad boom of the nineteenth century. Rich and powerful railroad barons wanted government subsidies for their projects: after all, they argued, they were serving the economy and the public good. Lobbyists had learned the ropes; they had schmoozed the main officials in the administration: it made sense to subcontract this work to them. Other groups over time were to lobby for punitive tariffs on imported textiles or to see safety or environmental regulation eased.

Lobbying has become a multi-billion-dollar industry: critics say it enables entrenched interest-groups to 'buy' the legislation that they want. They don't generally do it outright, of course, but by plying the already powerful with freebie-trips and lavish gifts, they can have a powerfully persuasive impact on the way we are all governed. Under George W. Bush, it's been alleged, more than 100 onetime lobbyists were appointed to regulators' roles, supposedly policing the activities of industries for which they were formerly paid advocates. Yet Obama's promise to exclude all lobbyists from his administration has hardly stood up to scrutiny.

But then, that's part of the problem. One man's lobbyist is another's fighter for justice. President Truman put it in almost so many words. Asked by a reporter whether he'd object to lobbyists who were

Albert Fall, former Secretary of the Interior is pictured here leaving court in 1929 – he was found guilty of bribery and received a sentence of one year in prison and a fine of $100,000 ($1.28 million today).

working for his programme, he replied: 'We probably wouldn't call those people lobbyists. We would call them citizens working in the public interest.'

Sexual Politics

Few would argue with Henry Kissinger's claim that 'power is the great aphrodisiac'. It acts on both the office-holder and on potential sexual partners. What we see in workplaces is replicated in the White House: the boss has allure – and some ability to compel. Some women may see a tryst with a President as a triumph – if sex is a competition, that's not surprising. Others may see the Oval Office couch as the quickest way to influence; others yet may feel they're romantically 'rescuing' a man they see as misunderstood.

Not that the President is innocent in such cases, easy as it is to see how one could let oneself be

Lobbyists Jack Abramoff and Michael Scanlon made millions of dollars – mainly from Native American communities who had sought their assistance in dealing with the legislature – by massively overbilling clients and bribing politicians.

> Someone who's made his life's work winning over crowds of hostile voters isn't going to be held up for long by the resistance of someone he's identified as a sexual target.

carried away with these particular privileges of power. The man with the world at his feet is, of course, only too likely to feel he has its women at his beck and call, and his office gives him a glamour he might not otherwise have possessed. That said, the glamour may well be real. A successful politician is often as not a natural charmer, a seducer skilled at swaying other individuals to his will – and a US President is by definition a *very* successful politician. Someone who's made his life's work winning over crowds of hostile voters isn't going to be held up for long by the resistance of someone he's identified as a sexual target

– unless that person has great strength of will herself.

Or *himself*, because although up to now all America's Presidents have been men, so too have several Presidential lovers. What Oscar Wilde notoriously called 'the love that dare not speak its name' has certainly kept very quiet in the official annals of the Presidency, but in some cases at least it does seem to have been there. There are historical health-warnings to be heeded: men were more openly affectionate toward each other in the nineteenth century than they've since become; they were far easier-going about things like sharing beds. And then there's the question of how far it's safe to talk of anyone being 'gay' – or even 'homosexual' – at a time when those very concepts did not exist.

All very true, and yet today's gay campaigners are understandably impatient of what they see as attempts to use such scholarly scruples to blind us to facts they feel are staring us in the face. Does the fact that the unmarried James Buchanan played house with Franklin Pierce's Vice President William Rufus King for 15 years prove conclusively that he was 'gay'? Of course it doesn't, but it sure creates some suspicions. And if Buchanan seems a bit minor, an also-ran in the great Presidential race, how about George Washington and Abraham Lincoln? The evidence in these cases is more circumstantial still, but it's been persistent: some rumours simply will not go away.

'I did not have sexual relations with that woman,' Bill Clinton insisted, but Monica Lewinsky disagreed. A semen-stained dress belonging to the intern clinched the case, though the President survived impeachment proceedings in 1998.

Dark, Not Depressing

Considering all these temptations, the surprise is that more Presidents haven't painted the White House black as sin, but that elegant residence has certainly seen some goings-on. The truth has been anything but edifying at times: abuse of power is as old as the United States, corruption as American as apple pie.

Yet there's no point in being pessimistic or overly depressed: if the 'City on a Hill' has often been a Babylon, it surely does us good to recognize our limitations. And to enjoy the spectacle as it unfolds in these pages, for if the history of the US Presidency has been a great deal darker than we may imagine, it's also been much more colourful than we assume.

FOUNDING FATHERS: SLAVEHOLDERS AND ADULTERERS

American history started as it meant to go on – as big and bold in its faults as in its virtues. Along with the glory there was graft, including dope-smoking and sexual shenanigans: the Founding Fathers were colossal figures, but with feet of clay.

'Liberty, when it begins to take root, is a plant of rapid growth.'

America's first four Presidents had all been signatories to the Declaration of Independence in 1776. The United States quite literally wouldn't have existed without them. They were great men – no-one would question that. But even great men may have flaws – and George Washington, John Adams, Thomas Jefferson and James Madison were no exception. When you add the immense confusion of the times into the general moral mix, you see how great the temptations must

With Washington burning and British invaders threatening the White House in 1812, Dolley Madison rescued the Declaration of Independence (left). She also saved a celebrated portrait of America's first President, George Washington (above).

have been: in a situation without precedent, these men were making it up as they went along.

They had, after all, just staged the first revolution of the modern age, and after such convulsions it takes a nation time to settle down. (Thankfully, the sins of the Founding Fathers were to pale into insignificance beside those of the French Revolutionaries, whose Reign of Terror, 1793–4 cost up to 40,000 lives.) When we see them now, in patriotic paintings, we see a group united in noble resolution, but it's really only in hindsight that this is so. They were courageous; and for certain, they fought together, but they had to overcome a great many reservations and rivalries. They had differences of opinion and competing ambitions; they came from a variety of backgrounds and couldn't always understand the attitudes of their comrades. There was a huge amount at stake: if the United States was as yet an insignificant little slip of a nation, it already had a superpower's sense of destiny.

GEORGE WASHINGTON, 1789–97

George Washington's place in the pantheon of heroes is secure, so there can be no harm in considering some of his shortcomings. Which is just as well, given that some of the things he did in the course of his career wouldn't necessarily have gone down so well with those who oversee our representatives' conduct nowadays. No one's ever suggested he was some kind of monster in the manner of Stalin or Genghis Khan; neither is there any serious question as to whether he deserves the honour due to his nation's founder. It's just that, sad to say, his reputation remains tarnished by behaviour which somehow doesn't seem quite worthy of such a man.

And it goes well beyond the great cherry-tree scandal of his childhood years. That is one crime of which, the historians say, he almost certainly wasn't guilty: Mason Weems seems to have made this story up, for the sake of colour and moral instruction, when he wrote his myth-making biography of the great man in 1800. It's a memorable story, of course, and as far as it goes it's not implausible – the kind of thing that might easily have happened, even if it didn't.

But many of us who 'cannot tell a lie' at six find that it gets easier as we get older – partly because we

---

> As no pecuniary consideration could have tempted me to accept this arduous employment, I do not wish to make any profit from it.

---

find newer, more creative ways of misleading others. We have no reason to believe that, as President, Washington ever stood up and spoke untruthfully to the people or their representatives. Even so, he was dogged by what we would nowadays call the 'character issue'.

The Padding Problem

'First in war'? Undoubtedly. It's easy to forget how close to final defeat the colonists came after the reverse at Brandywine in 1777 and the appalling winter that followed at Valley Forge. Washington saw them through, and emerged from the fighting to be 'first in peace' – a shoo-in as the United States' inaugural President – and 'first in the hearts of his countrymen' for all time. But did he have to be first with his expenses claims as well? Especially when he'd made such a self-sacrificing performance of agreeing to lead the Continental Army without pay? 'As no pecuniary consideration could have tempted me to accept this arduous employment, I do not wish to make any profit from it,' he assured a grateful Congress.

Little did they know what they were letting themselves in for. If Washington was a doughty

Left: As craggy as his Mount Rushmore face, America's first President looks the picture of integrity in this contemporary engraving. In some ways, sadly, the reality fell short of the idealized image.

Right: With her rose and her roguish glance, Sally Fairfax shows the face, the figure and the personality that captured Washington's heart. But how much more was there to their relationship really than a high-flown crush?

George Washington chats with a (white) farmhand as the harvest is brought in on his estate. It's easy to forget, presented with this idyllic scene, that the black workers are all slaves and that the democracy he'd helped found was firmly rooted in racism and oppression.

warrior, he was also a filer of expense claims on an epic scale. Nothing was too good for the nation's protector: a band to play to him on his birthday? A fancy leather letter-case? If Washington wanted it, he got it – and Congress couldn't bat an eyelid. In his eight years as commander, from 1775 to 1783, he claimed just under $450,000 ($9.4 million today) in *personal* expenses – an incredible sum in eighteenth-century terms.

And it wasn't just that he was extravagant: many of the claims had little or no documentation – some of these were for tens of thousands of dollars at a time.

> Well into the winter at Valley Forge, when his troops in their thousands were literally starving, he was banqueting on beef, veal, pigeons, chickens, oysters ... you name it.

Washington became masterly in his wielding of weasel-words like 'sundries', whilst he makes the use of 'etc' into something of an art form. Other claims were for 'loans' to friends – never repaid: was Washington looking after his supporters at the state's expense, or lining his own pockets? Sometimes the latter conclusion is just about impossible to avoid. Could he *really* have spent $800 ($23,000 today) on saddles?

His greed was all-consuming – not just financial avarice but rampant gluttony. Whatever the circumstances, the commander of the Republican army always insisted on eating (dare one say it?) like a king. Well into the winter at Valley Forge, when his troops in their thousands were literally starving, he was banqueting on beef, veal, pigeons, chickens, oysters ... you name it; and washing it down with the finest imported wines.

Obscene? Well, yes – though Washington genuinely doesn't seem to have seen any inconsistency; and

OUT OF THE FRYING PAN ... ?

GIVEN HOW HARD and heroically Washington fought against the British, could it really be possible that – as some of his opponents claimed – he was closer to the old country than he had any business being? Some suggested that he was not committed to republican ideals, and that he even planned to establish an American monarchy. It's quite true that he had a highly developed sense of his own importance – the expenses scandal is testimony to that. He took his office as President extremely seriously too: he expected visitors to stay standing in his presence. And he had his inauguration carried out with what many felt was rather un-republican pomp. 'I fear we may have exchanged George the Third for George the First,' one senator whispered to his neighbour in the crowd.

there's no doubt that he was conscientious in his own way. He threw himself into his general's duties, working round the clock to keep up morale among his men. He seems to have taken literally the idea that his own welfare as leader was paramount; the well-being of his army would ultimately flow from that.

Not surprisingly, when the war was over, and he had been asked to be his country's President, Washington offered to carry on serving 'unpaid'. Equally unsurprisingly, Congress quietly turned him down, awarding him a $25,000 ($520,000 today) salary instead. A princely sum, but a bargain after the 'pro bono' bonanza of the war years.

Marriage and Martha

Martha Dandridge Custis was a widow in her twenties when she

First in the heart of her husband? Martha Dandridge Custis may have become her country's first First Lady, but some historians have suggested that she came a poor second to Sally Fairfax in Washington's affections.

first caught Washington's attention – though it's widely believed that the future President had eyes only for her estate. From her late husband, Daniel Parke Custis, she had inherited extensive properties in land and slaves at White House Plantation, New Kent County, Virginia. Washington was widely believed to be in love with a certain Sally Fairfax: he wrote her romantic (if ambiguous) letters, in which he confessed himself a 'votary of Love'. Local gossips were in no doubt that they had consummated their affair. Many modern historians are more doubtful. Were the tongue-waggers putting two and two together and making five? Or are the academic sceptics trying too hard to defend the honour of the Founding Father? In the end, we can only follow our own hunches here.

Whatever the attraction, Washington having married Martha in 1759, she became America's first First Lady 30 years later. A loving wife and loyal companion, she deserves credit for the time she spent on campaign with her soldier husband – though, as we've

seen, conditions for Washington and his staff weren't exactly Spartan.

There is another rumour that puts us on even shakier ground – that future Treasury Secretary Alexander Hamilton was Washington's son: he was born in 1755 (or, more likely, 1757) on the island of Nevis in the West Indies. His acknowledged father James Hamilton and mother Rachel Fawcett Lavien both belonged to wealthy planter families there: we have no reason to believe that Washington was in Nevis at the relevant time – or, for that matter, ever. It's true that he'd been in Barbados accompanying his brother Lawrence when he was recuperating after illness, but this had been a few years before – and some 579km (360 miles) away. It's true, though (and very likely a source for a great deal of the speculation) that when the young Alexander joined Washington's staff, the General said he loved him 'like a son'. Some have even speculated on the existence of a homosexual

Whatever reservations we might have about his character, Washington's courage and resourcefulness weren't in doubt. He'd established his military reputation as a brave young captain in the French and Indian War of 1754–63.

relationship between them – this is at least more likely than that the younger man was the elder's son.

Sleeping with the Enemy?

In 1776, Thomas Hickey, a member of Washington's bodyguard was arrested in New York: it was alleged that he was a British loyalist, and that he'd conspired to kidnap his commander. The committee charged with investigating the case was alarmed to find witness after witness confirming in the course of its inquiries that Washington was accustomed to visit a certain house beside the Hudson River late at night, his appearance always heavily disguised. It seemed that the general had a mistress, Mary Gibbons, of whom he

An indispensable aide during the Revolutionary War, Alexander Hamilton was to serve as President Washington's Treasury Secretary. Some speculated that he had been his mentor's lover – or even that he was his bastard son.

was 'very fond' and whom he 'maintained … very genteelly' there. More shocking than the moral question was the claim that Mary had been accustomed carefully to going through her lover's papers while he slept and copying items of special interest to be sold on to the British. Hickey was hanged regardless, but the full facts of the conspiracy (if that's what it was) were never discovered. Was Washington really the victim of a Loyalist Mata Hari, or was this story just a smear put about by his pro-British enemies?

The French Connection

The impact of the American Revolution on the world was simply shattering. It is acknowledged as the immediate inspiration for the uprising that overthrew the monarchy in France in 1789. But there was a revolutionary two-way street, because although America was ultimately first in striking against its oppressors, sedition had already been seething in France for quite some time. When America's moment came, radicals in France were watching carefully, and some crossed the Atlantic to help in the fight for liberty. The most famous of these,

ROPE AND DOPE

DID GEORGE WASHINGTON smoke marijuana? There's every reason to think he did: dope-smoking didn't carry any of the stigma it has today. And hemp, the crop from whose harvested leaves the drug is derived, was grown everywhere across the American South: it was easy to grow, and its fibrous stems were useful for making everything from rope to cloth and paper. A notorious journal entry dating from 1765 finds Washington lamenting that he's missed the moment for separating his male from his female plants – this matters only because it's the females which are good for smoking.

Gilbert du Motier, Marquis de Lafayette, was an aristocrat and incredibly well-connected – he first heard of the colonists' quarrel at dinner with the brother of King George III.

Impressed by his commitment, Congress awarded him the rank of major-general and they sent him to assist George Washington as *aide-de-camp*. There seems to have been some hope that this mark of preferment would send a signal to France, which would respond with military support. This was not as naive as it might sound, for if France's monarchy had no obvious interest in fostering revolutionary resistance, it had a clear incentive to see its English enemy done down. Thanks to Lafayette's personal diplomacy, indeed, during a brief return to his homeland in the spring of 1777, French support was ultimately forthcoming.

Love and Attachment
In the danger and excitement of war, bonds between men may form quickly and intensely: soon the glamorous French Marquis and the American General

No one did more than the Baron von Steuben to drill the Continental Army or train up its officers tactically. He was a military man, and a man's man; we would say these days that he was gay.

were fast friends. Washington wrote fulsomely to his friend of his 'love and attachment', was desolate when he had to return to France and wept with emotion when they were reunited. Was their love expressed more physically? The record is sufficiently ambiguous for generations of historians to have doubted this – but were they what we would now describe as being 'in denial'?

A great many gay scholars think so now. They point to the fact that evidence shows that sexual relationships among men appear to have passed all but unnoticed at this time. Washington's Chief of Staff, the Prussian-born Baron von Steuben, never married and left his estate to two young aides he'd become close to through years of campaigning. Few now doubt that theirs was a sexual relationship as well.

JOHN ADAMS, 1797–1801

George Washington having been directly awarded the position, John Adams has the distinction of having been the first man ever *elected* to the US Presidency. But there's little indication that he appreciated the importance of this historic honour. Despite a theoretical commitment to democracy, the sort of high-minded gentlemen who formed America's political elite in this period were still inclined to despise the vulgar business of appealing to the great unwashed for their support. For the lead-in to the election of 1796, Adams – far from going out on the stump, pressing flesh and kissing babies – simply shut himself away in his home in Quincy, Massachusetts.

The United States – a helpless diplomatic virgin – is no match for French negotiators in this cartoonist's view of the XYZ Affair. America could ill afford to spend huge sums on bribes – but it could afford a full-blown conflict even less.

He insisted with a fastidious shudder you can almost feel 'I am determined to be a Silent Spectator of the silly and the wicked Game.'

He would play no active part in the campaign but insisted with a fastidious shudder you can almost feel: 'I am determined to be a Silent Spectator of the silly and the wicked Game.'

Not surprisingly, then, Adams didn't make any inroads on the Southern heartlands of Jefferson, his main opponent, but New England's support was enough to see him safely home. His Presidency, if truth be told, offers meagre pickings for the searcher after scandal, though it wasn't short on excitement of a sort. By 1798, there was fighting at sea between

FEDERALISTS VS REPUBLICANS

MODERN CONCEPTS OF 'LEFT' AND 'RIGHT' are of limited value when it comes to comprehending the politics of America in these early decades. In today's terms, indeed, the Republicans were – quite radically – on the left. Thomas Jefferson, their leader and hero, was self-consciously a man of the Enlightenment and a revolutionary in the French mould. The principles of monarchy and aristocracy were to be stamped out and religion was to be kept strictly separated from state interference – just as politics was to be kept free from interference by the clergy. Freedom was the Republican battle cry, but it had yet to become attached to the idea of market economics: Republicans held big business in deep suspicion; the sturdy small farmer was held up as the quintessential American.

The Federalists, very briefly, were keen to place effective management before high ideals. This was better conducted at state than at national level, they believed. Government's role was to see to the security of the country and the soundness of the economy, enabling American manufacturers, merchants and traders to get on with their work. Not surprisingly, this philosophy took root in Massachusetts and other states of New England where industrialization was well under way, whilst Republicanism prevailed in the agrarian South.

America and France. The revolutionary government in that country was enraged by US refusal to pay back loans made by the now-deposed monarchy.

Three French agents, Jean Conrad Hottinguer, Pierre Bellamy and Lucien Hauteval, were entrusted with the negotiations: they were known publicly as X, Y and Z. As the price of peace, they demanded a repayment of $250,000 ($4.5 million today) to France; a further 'loan' of $100 million (more than one billion dollars today); and a $250,000 ($4.5 million today) sum for French Foreign Minister Charles Maurice de Talleyrand (basically a bribe). America's weakness after its years of fighting was only too obvious to the outside world: hence this resort to shakedown diplomacy on France's part. The French captured 300 US ships before the X, Y, Z Affair blew over.

The Last Laugh
Adams was forced to be a bit of a silent spectator throughout this undignified episode, but he had the last laugh when the Republicans overplayed their hand. Having raised a clamour to have France's demands revealed to the public, they succeeded in humiliating the President – but they themselves suffered from the inevitable backlash against the French. What emerged about their cynical bullying rebounded badly on the Republicans, who were still strongly associated with the values of the French Revolution.

John Adams despised the democratic process that had made him America's first elected President. But, in taking his self-conscious stand 'above' the hurly-burly of everyday politics, he lost touch with the workings of his own administration.

Criminalizing Opposition

Adams was something of a spectator too in the other scandal to shake his administration: it seems to have been his allies rather than he himself who introduced the Naturalization and Sedition Acts. Both had reasonable-sounding justifications: the first decreed that new immigrants would have to wait longer (14 years) before they got the vote; that way, they would show their true commitment to the United States. A couple of associated Alien Acts meanwhile gave the government sweeping powers to deport those immigrants they believed were plotting against the state. This was all very well – except that the record clearly showed that new immigrants were more likely to support the Republicans than the Federalists.

The second act included in its definition of 'sedition' the publication of any 'false, scandalous and malicious writing' against the government or its

> So often in history, we've seen revolution leading inexorably to repression: just how narrowly the American Revolution avoided this fate is not always appreciated.

officials. As the Republicans weren't slow to see, this could be interpreted by a Federalist government to cover criticism of just about any kind. So often in history, we've seen revolution leading inexorably to repression: just how narrowly the American Revolution avoided this fate is not always appreciated. Sure, there was never anything remotely comparable to the French Terror, but these Acts attempted to enshrine it in law that opposition was treasonous.

But Adams lost the election of 1800: Jefferson's victorious Republicans lost no time in reversing the legislation and pardoning and recompensing all those who had suffered under it. For the Federalists, this attack on freedom was going to take some living down.

The USS *Constellation* battles it out with a French warship in the naval hostilities that accompanied the XYZ Affair. Fortunately, the episode ended up a mere scandal: the new republic could hardly have coped with a major war.

THOMAS JEFFERSON, 1801–9

Even by Presidential standards, Thomas Jefferson was a star. He cast lustre on the Presidency, rather than it on him. A brilliant man of boundless energy, in between fighting for freedom and drafting constitutions, he did important work in everything from archaeology to architecture, from palaeontology to gardening. He extended America (doubling it in size) with the Louisiana Purchase and sent the Lewis and Clark exhibition out to map the West. But he did other things as well, and not all of them were quite so seemly. Nor do they sit so easily, from today's perspective, with his ideals.

A Duel for Democracy

Anyone who hadn't realized how high the stakes were becoming in US politics was in for a rude awakening on 11 July 1804. The shots that rang out at dawn that day across the empty woods of the Heights of Weehawken, New Jersey, were to echo through the American system for decades. Jefferson's Vice President, Aaron Burr, had just killed the Federalist former Secretary of the Treasury, Alexander Hamilton: the political had become personal in no uncertain terms.

The idea of the duel to the death as a means of settling private quarrels on questions of honour might be assumed to belong to the Old World, whose aristocratic young men

No man is bigger than the office of US President, but it might be said that Thomas Jefferson came close. The greatest statesman of his day, he was an idealist, an intellectual and a scientist of repute.

> As for Burr, some who spoke to him after concluded that he'd fired in fear and shock; others that he was a cold-blooded murderer, for his foe was finally to bleed to death.

still saw themselves as belonging to a special class of knightly warriors. Prussian *junkers* might duel with sabres; even English lords with fighting foils; but what business did the leaders of the world's first modern nation have with such goings-on? No matter; as we've already seen, democratic values had only partly taken root: the American elite still saw themselves as gentlemen, and had the pride to match. America found itself caught betwixt and between in its attitudes at this time: duelling had just been declared illegal in New Jersey and New York. But there was still a great deal of sympathy for those who, feeling their honour had been impugned, decided to take the law into their own hands.

Burr and Hamilton had never managed to make things up since the campaign of 1800: this had been no-holds-barred, and neither side had spared the other. Rather than calming down after the election race was run, however, they'd continued to nurse grievances against each other. Told by Thomas Jefferson that he'd be looking for another running-mate for his second term, the Vice President had run for the post of Governor of

New York in 1804. His opponent, Philip Schuyler, was Hamilton's father-in-law. The sometime Treasury Secretary pitched in with a will. Penning a series of scathing articles, he didn't succeed in stopping Burr's election, but he did succeed in irritating him beyond endurance. When further remarks were made on both sides, and neither showed any willingness to withdraw them, it was agreed that the two would fight a duel.

What would seem to be a simple exchange of shots actually ended in complete confusion. Hamilton fired one shot and it went wide. He subsequently said he'd deliberately missed, but this may have been his bid to save his pride – or, alternatively, a chillingly calculated attempt to destroy the reputation of Burr, whose shot at him

Jefferson's first administration was rocked by one of US political history's more unusual scandals, when Vice President Aaron Burr killed the former Treasury Secretary Alexander Hamilton in a duel at Weehawken, New Jersey.

struck home. Hamilton had far more firearms experience, and he doesn't appear to have explained to his opponent how hard the hair-trigger pistols he had brought would be to use. As for Burr, some who spoke to him after concluded that he'd fired in fear and shock; others that he was a cold-blooded murderer, for his wounded foe was finally to bleed to death.

Burr was indicted for murder and fled. In Washington, however, he was safely outside the jurisdiction of New York, so he was able to complete his Vice Presidency in peace.

Religion and Radicalism

The obvious objection to Jefferson, in the eyes of his contemporaries, was his often-articulated disdain for organized religion. Like many modern-minded intellectuals of his time, Jefferson was a 'deist' – he believed that there was an originating divinity, a 'first cause' which set the universal order going, but did not accept that this deity took a continuing interest in the affairs of his creation. This theology (if it can be called that) accounted for the existence of the world but dispensed with most of what we think of as religion.

A French diplomat dances in delight as, 'stung' by a Napoleonic hornet, prairie dog President Jefferson coughs up quantities of gold for western Florida. James Akin's 1804 cartoon takes the popular view that Jefferson's land purchases had been bad bargains.

> From his point of view, as long as the nation's small farmers kept sowing and reaping, the country would be able to feed itself.

Out one day, when out with his like-minded friend Philip Mazzei, Jefferson saw a ruined church and wisecracked 'Good enough for him born in a stable.' The story got out and reached the press: it scandalized Americans that their President could speak so slightingly of their Saviour.

They were scarcely less shocked when Jefferson invited Thomas Paine to pay a visit to America. In fairness, the English-born radical was owed a profound

The PRAIRIE DOG sickened at the sting of the HORNET — or a Diplomatic Puppet exhibiting his Deceptions!

THE PRESIDENT'S LADY

THE HISTORY OF THE US PRESIDENCY was as yet only a short one, but already there was a well-defined role for the First Lady. This left Thomas Jefferson in a difficult position. His wife Martha had died in 1782, long before his election to the Presidency. What was he to do? The solution wasn't far to find: he looked to Dolley Madison, the wife of his Secretary of State. She was renowned as one of Washington's most accomplished hostesses, so she was fully equal to the task of entertaining visiting dignitaries and welcoming their wives.

Did she perform other traditional wifely duties for the President? So his political opponents would have us believe. They hinted darkly at a sex scandal in the White House. And they didn't stop there. In their eagerness to damage Dolley's husband James Madison, they suggested that he and Jefferson were pimping out Dolley and her sister Anna to potential political allies, to gain their support.

The First Lady who never was, Martha Wayles Skelton married Thomas Jefferson in 1772. Despite poor health, she had borne him six children by the time she died, just 10 years later, leaving her husband prostrated with grief.

debt by the United States. Not only had the author of *The Rights of Man* (1791) been an inspiration to the leaders of the American Revolution but he had come in person to play his part in the fight for freedom. Since that time, however, things had moved on: the United States was establishing itself as a stable democracy but Paine's firebrand rhetoric had shown no signs of cooling. With the shocking example of the French Terror always before them, most Americans did not feel like 'revolutionaries' any more. When the Federalist press painted Paine as a blood-soaked monster, their readers didn't really take a great deal of persuading.

Locking Out Trade

Jefferson did for his own second term by one of the most self-defeating laws ever passed in American history: the Embargo Act of 1807. This prohibited the import or export of all goods to foreign ports. Political in motivation, it was intended to uphold US neutrality in the war that was by this time raging between Great Britain and Napoleonic France. This policy was probably 'correct' as far as it went, but it took no account of economic realities. Then again, Jefferson took a revolutionary's pride in his indifference to issues of industry and trade. From his point of view, as long as the nation's small farmers kept sowing and reaping, the country would be able to feed itself. What else would any idealistic American want?

Well, idealistic or not, those in the industrialized North wanted a great deal more. In particular, they wanted to be able to trade, to bring in raw materials and ship out the products of their manufactories. The legislation was unenforceable: goods were taken to

Canada and then quietly brought across the border, or smuggled in by fishing boats all the way down the eastern seaboard. But industry and trade still suffered: New York came close to seceding from the Union, such was the crisis it was undergoing. Jefferson was finally forced to lift the embargo, but he did not do so until 1809, just a few days before his Presidency reached its end.

Agent 13

James Wilkinson was a war hero: he'd fought bravely and resourcefully in the War of Independence. But he was also a traitor of the basest kind. Others might betray their country out of misguided idealism or maddened by some grievance, real or imagined, but Wilkinson did it because it was worth his while. In the aftermath of the Louisiana Purchase, as American settlers poured west into the Mississippi Valley, he bought up furs and produce, loaded them on to a raft and set off downriver. He made it as far as New Orleans, where he sold his cargo at a considerable profit and sold his loyalty to the Spanish at a still larger one. He may have been a soldier, but he was a wheeler-dealer and a charmer too: seasoned politicians

Below: As viewed by the makers of the movie *Jefferson in Paris* (1995), Thomas's relationship with Sally Hemings was a loving if complex one. His critics claim that it was at least implicitly coercive from first to last.

Right: Seen here haloed by the radiance of revolutionary optimism, Tom Paine was as often portrayed as a fire-breathing monster of mob-rule. For President Jefferson, though, he was always an inspiration and a friend.

Modern America's multiracial spirit is inspiringly embodied in the assembled descendants of Sally Hemings and Jefferson. Yet important questions about the nature of the relationship between landowner and slave-girl still remain.

were as putty in his hands. He enjoyed the favour first of Washington, then of Adams and of Jefferson – though rumours of his dodgy dealings kept coming in. As a highly placed officer in the military – and ultimately as Jefferson's Governor of Northern Louisiana – he was privy to secrets of great value to the state. None of his Presidential masters seems to have wanted to believe that such shameless treachery

as this could be conceivable, however. Not until James Madison's Presidency would he be brought to book. In 1811, he was brought to book at last – but even now he managed to wriggle his way out and was acquitted. In 1813–14, he fell under suspicion again, when two campaigns against the Spanish came to nothing. This time, too, however, he was cleared by an inquiry. Only after his death in 1825 was it finally confirmed that he had been an agent (Agent 13) of the Spanish all along.

Slaves in the Family
The Father of American Democracy was a literal father too: Jefferson's first family took its place

among the new republic's patrician class. But then, it seems, there was a second family: after Martha's death in 1782, Thomas embarked on a secret liaison. Several aspects of the relationship with Sally Hemings set alarm-bells ringing for us in the twenty-first century. For one thing, she was just 14 when it all began. She was also an African-American slave-girl: you'd wonder now how truly consensual such an affair could be, given that one party was the property of the other.

It's a reminder, of course, of how morally blind even the best of us can be: Jefferson's idealism and love of freedom cannot seriously be doubted. Yet somehow, what his friend Tom Paine called the 'Rights of Man' weren't deemed to apply to men of a different colour – or, for that matter, to women of either race. Democracy has always been a luxury for the

Not much more than a generation into its history, the American dream of democracy seemed to be going up in flames when invading British forces set fire to the White House in 1812. The interior was destroyed and much of the exterior was charred.

> She was just 14 when it all began. She was also an African-American slave-girl: you'd wonder now how truly consensual such an affair could be, given that one party was the property of the other.

privileged, it might be said: ancient Athens, notoriously, was kept going by slave labour. And in America to this day, the poorest sections of the population tend not to take part in the democratic process – though they're admittedly self-disenfranchised, defeated by fatalistic apathy. All the Founding Fathers spoke up for freedom, though it doesn't appear to have occurred to any of them that this right might legitimately be claimed by so many thousands of African-American slaves. It still seems shocking that Jefferson, the most conspicuously

idealistic of all the men of 1776, should have accepted this situation quite so unquestioningly.

But then such relationships were woven into the very pattern of Southern life. Sally's mother had herself been sired by an English sea-captain on an unknown African woman. Having come into the household as part of Martha's property, Sally was almost certainly her mistress's half-sister – such were the secret ties that bound in this society. Whether you see it as a good thing or a bad thing, Jefferson's relationship with Sally was certainly enduring: it went on for 38 years and produced seven children.

JAMES MADISON, 1809–17

James Madison, by profession a lawyer, will always have his place in America's political hall of fame: no one did more than he to compose the Constitution – or to explain it. As a practical politician, though, he ultimately fell short: his Presidency definitely wasn't America's finest hour. It was on his watch that Americans endured the ignominy of seeing the White House burned down by British troops. Worse, the War

of 1812 was – quite justifiably – called 'Mr Madison's War'. The Royal Navy had been harassing American shipping for some time – chiefly because it was trading with Britain's bitter enemy, France. The British also refused to recognize the right of deserting seamen to become American citizens: it stopped US vessels to 'press' such men into naval service.

Even so, there was no need for Madison to rise to these provocations. He chose to do so because he thought America could fight and win. The young hotheads on his staff believed an attack on British North America (now Canada) would be a walkover, because the British presence on the ground there was so thin. Madison put far more effort into preparing the political path to war than he did into making ready his military. When battle was joined, the tiny, underfunded and ill-equipped American militia soon found themselves in a hopeless situation. Though

Satirical attacks on the 'Presidentress' and her power, while plainly reflecting the misogyny of many in the political class, were at the same time aimed at Madison himself, perceived as too weak for such high office.

A POOR SPECIMEN

THE SMALLEST AND SLIGHTEST of US Presidents to date, James Madison stood only 1.62 m (5ft 4in) or so and he never weighed more than 45kg (100lbs). As though to balance out his mental stature, his physical presence was weak and puny. He was quiet and impassive in his manner, a cold fish. But as if this buttoned-up persona wasn't enough, James Madison suffered fits: he would suddenly be frozen into immobility, as though by a seizure. His condition was indeed diagnosed as epilepsy by the doctors of the day, though experts today prefer to characterize it as 'epileptoid hysteria', because it is believed to have a psychological dimension. It's easy to see it as a direct expression by the body of a helplessness being experienced by the mind. For Madison, having been badly afflicted by the condition in his youth, seems to have 'snapped out of it' spontaneously when he found his political vocation. Only in the 1800s did Dolley find her husband 'freezing' again, at a time when the Royal Navy was attacking American ships with virtual impunity: Madison was literally paralyzed by his inability to act, it seemed.

the British forces in Canada were still smaller, they had vastly more experience than the Americans and quickly overcame them. Meanwhile, the Royal Navy was cleaning up at sea. Picking off American ships more or less at will, it also blockaded the eastern ports, bringing economic life grinding slowly to a halt.

Washington in Flames

The attack on Washington of 1814 was more of symbolic than of military significance – but what a symbol! The White House and the Capitol up in flames! The only glimmer of light in the enveloping darkness was the red glare of the rockets at Baltimore – whose successful defence would inspire America's national

anthem. But Britain, by now, was flagging: North America was far away and Napoleon's France was occupying its energies in Europe. So Madison appeared to have got away with one of the greatest foreign-policy mistakes in US history – though posterity has been a sterner judge.

But then, to look on the bright side, it was the perfect opportunity to rebuild the smoke-blackened White House. The present Palladian pile was the result. And in Dolley Madison, America had the right First Lady for the job of bringing the new building to completion. America's hostess with the mostest was also its most indefatigable interior designer. She took charge of the whole thing, with as keen an eye for budgetary constraints as for elegance and fashion. At last! An undisputed triumph of the Madison administration!

James Madison looks every inch the statesman here – assured and authoritative – but the contemporary engraving offers no hint of the ceaseless struggle America's Fourth President had to 'hold things together', mentally and physically.

WASHINGTON AS A FREEMASON.

MADE A MASON 1752. COMMANDER OF THE AMERICAN ARMY, 1775. PRESIDENT OF THE UNITED STATES, 1789.

CORRUPT CONSOLIDATION

America came of age in corruption: their country's survival assured, her statesmen got on with the business of lining their pockets and bolstering their power. Electors soon grew cynical and yet, low as their expectations were, their politicians still found new and original ways of disappointing them.

'The best form of government is that which is most likely to prevent the greatest sum of evil.'

The ruins of the White House might still have been gently smouldering, but the danger seemed to have passed. America had secured its liberty, and could now look forward to the future. There was a perceptible calming of political nerves as the new nation entered what became known as the 'Era of Good Feeling'. Political differences didn't go away – neither, of course, did political scandals – but overall America felt pretty good about itself.

Like many of his generation, George Washington (left) had been a freemason, but politics was itself becoming a thing of secret cliques. The election of William Henry Harrison (above) owed less to democratic appeal than to his supporters' working of the system.

JAMES MONROE, 1817–25

James Monroe was actually a Founding Father. He had fought in the Revolutionary War. Indeed, he can be seen holding up the flag in the famous painting *Washington Crossing the Delaware*. But his Presidency seems to belong to a different age, one in which America had put its early growing pains behind it and was pushing forward, a young but well-established nation. Monroe deserves much of the credit for that himself: easy-going and affable, with opponents as well as allies, he would bend over backwards to avoid conflict or cross words. The world-changing rhetoric of the freedom struggle long abandoned, Monroe now argued for a politics of the least worst option: 'The best form of government is that which is most likely to prevent the greatest sum of evil.'

It hadn't always been so. As a hot-headed young idealist, he'd been a huge admirer of the French Revolution and had got himself sent as the United

States' ambassador to Paris. He had fallen foul of George Washington's more conservative approach, however, and found himself increasingly isolated. Left out of the loop in 1794, when the United States signed the Jay Treaty with England, he was recalled to

> Monroe's adminstration was dogged by a series of scandals which, though petty, left the government of America looking sullied.

America not long after, Washington claiming he hadn't been up to the job. There was no 'good feeling' in the furious Monroe's response as he condemned what he called this 'dishonourable and unmanly attack of our insane President'.

A Culture of Corruption

Whether he was insane or not, Washington certainly knew what he was doing when he filed his expenses, as we've seen, and Monroe was happy enough to emulate his old adversary in this regard. Where Washington had lined his pockets in the field of war, however, Monroe did it during the battle to rebuild the White House (which was not yet completed), taking somewhat imaginative advantage of the

'Furniture Fund'. First, rather as Washington had, Monroe made a major point of his personal self-sacrifice: he sold his own furniture – at an astronomical profit – to a grateful nation. He then made lavish withdrawals from the fund for ongoing purchases, eventually leaving it $11,000 ($183,000 today) in the red.

The 'Era of Good Feeling' was beginning to leave a bad taste in the mouth. Monroe's administration was dogged by a series of scandals which, though petty,

NOT SO NICE

Down on the plantation, the feeling was anything but good. Monroe wasn't a believer in slavery – for what that was worth. He favoured its 'peaceful' phasing out – though he took no active steps to set any machinery for it in motion; nor did he say what existing slaves were to do till that happy conclusion had been brought about. Their master's humanitarian instincts could hardly be said to have done Monroe's own slaves a great deal of good. The President's money worries had more bearing on their lives. His

extravagant lifestyle and chronic indebtedness may have been a weight in his own mind, but the terrible physical burden fell on them. He'd been forced by debts to sell the family plantation before he became President, but had various other landholdings in the South. An absentee landlord, away in Washington, he – quite unrealistically – looked to these to see him through his financial problems: worked into the ground by brutal overseers, his slaves had to pay the price.

Above: The newly rebuilt and refurnished White House was a fitting emblem for the peace and prosperity of the 'Era of Good Feeling' – but there was ill-feeling about Monroe's management of its funding.

Right: His years as a revolutionary firebrand now well behind him, James Monroe had settled into a comfortable and conservative middle age – much like the nation over whose political life he now presided.

left the government of America looking sullied. Major Christopher Vandeventer, Clerk to John Calhoun, the Secretary of War, first brought the White House into disrepute when he allowed himself to be played by his unscrupulous brother-in-law, Elijah Mix. In 1818, trading on inside information, he bought up granite the government was going to have to use for building fortifications in Chesapeake Bay, then sold it on to the government at an inflated price. Vandeventer, incautiously, allowed himself to be 'cut' in for a quarter of the contract – while, crazily, Calhoun approved the deal.

Rival Tactics

The publication in 1823–4 of a series of articles above the byline 'A.B.' embarrassed the administration further, since they accused the Treasury Secretary,

Left: John Calhoun had a reputation for iron integrity, though this was badly damaged by the Elijah Mix scandal of 1818. If Monroe's Secretary of War wasn't actually criminal, he was criminally naïve.

Right: With accusations of corruption flying thick and fast, it was nice to actually find that the occasional one was unfounded: in 1824, a congressional inquiry cleared Treasury Secretary William H. Crawford of all wrongdoing.

William H. Crawford, of corruption. He had, it was claimed, far too cosy a relationship with the local banks he was using to raise tax revenues in the West. An inquiry exonerated Crawford: there is no doubt that the arrangements the government had made were rather ramshackle, but what was it to do in what was still very much frontier territory? 'A.B.' turned out to be the Illinois Senator Ninian Edwards, who'd set out deliberately to do a party rival down.

Brother Joe

One great American institution that can be seen to have begun during the Monroe Presidency was that of the embarrassing Presidential brother. Donald Nixon, Sam Houston Johnson, Billy Carter, and Roger Clinton all did their bit to undermine the dignity of their sibling's Presidencies, but the tradition starts with Joseph Jones Monroe. He kept running up debts, which his big brother felt he had to discharge on his behalf. Eventually, Joseph joined the rush of settlers to the West: it seems safe to assume that he had a bit of Presidential pressure to speed him on his way. He died in Howard County, Missouri, in 1824.

JOHN QUINCY ADAMS, 1825–9

John Quincy Adams was the son of Second President John Adams. His most lasting legacy, ironically, is known as the 'Monroe Doctrine'. As Secretary of State, Adams was the man who first formulated the view that the United States was entitled to police the whole of the Americas and to see any European interference as an act of aggression toward itself. A warning to the world in deceptively measured,

'diplomatic' language, it sums up neatly the character of a man who certainly wasn't anything like as meek or easy-going as he may have seemed.

That became remarkably clear in the unusual manner of his accession to the Presidency (to talk of his 'election' to the office seems misplaced). Many US Presidents could be said to have left office under a cloud; Quincy Adams was unusual because he actually started out that way. None of the five candidates had won an outright majority in the elections of 1824, though General Andrew Jackson had clearly had the largest share, with 43.1 per cent of the poll against Adams' 30.5 per cent. But, the lowest-scoring candidate, Henry Clay, having been forced to drop out of the race, he (an old adversary of Jackson's) threw his weight behind Adams, who was accordingly elected.

An American Monarchy?

Not surprisingly, Jackson and his supporters said that Adams had 'stolen' the Presidency. It was the end of the 'Era of Good Feeling'. Even those who didn't like Jackson much were uneasy that a President's son should have become President: they feared that some sort of European-style monarchical dynasty might be emerging.

John Quincy Adams' grand and haughty manner did nothing to disarm such critics. He showed no sign of humility as he embarked on a far-reaching, free-spending policy agenda. It wasn't that he was personally corrupt, but people didn't feel he had a

> Even those who didn't like Jackson much were uneasy that a President's son should have become President.

mandate for embarking upon an ambitious programme of improvements to infrastructure, including important road- and canal-building projects.

Neither were people won over by the way the President's two eldest sons behaved. George Washington Adams, a womanizer and alcoholic, was found drowned at 28 (he'd apparently committed suicide); John Adams

Above: It's Jackson and Adams (in the middle) neck-and-neck, with Crawford coming up third and Clay a dropout as the candidates race for the finish-line in David Johnston Claypoole's famous cartoon of the 1824 election.

Right: Louisa Adams may have had a regal air but beneath that poise was anxiety and illness. She suffered from migraines, miscarriages and frequent bouts of depression, in the course of her married life.

II was also an alcoholic. He too died young, at the age of only 31. With hindsight we might wonder whether the pressure of following so distinguished a grandfather and father might have proven too much for these young men. To their contemporaries, though, their behaviour seemed that of over-privileged crown princes.

Wedding and Wailing

When First Lady Louisa Adams' niece was orphaned, Mary Catherine Hellen was brought to live in the White House. Just 13, she was an ungovernable free spirit. Within two years, she had grown up into a rather frightening teenage *femme fatale*, driving her male cousins wild with lust and jealousy. Some sort of equilibrium seemed to have been established when she became engaged to George Washington Adams – though not before she'd broken the heart of his younger brother, Charles Francis Adams. But George dutifully agreed to postpone the marriage till he'd

THE TSAR AND THE CHAMBERMAID

John Quincy Adams had served as American Ambassador to Russia from 1809 to 1814. During this time one of his chambermaids made some flattering comments on Tsar Alexander I in a letter home. To break the ice at a meeting with the Russian ruler, the Ambassador had mentioned this. Charmed, Alexander had asked if he might be introduced to the young woman. The meeting that followed may well have been toe-curlingly embarrassing, but it was hardly sufficient grounds for the later accusation that John Quincy Adams had pimped out his servants to the Tsar. Still, Americans were slowly learning that all is fair, not only in love and war, but in the race for the White House too.

completed his education, leaving Mary in the White House, dangerously footloose.

John Adams II, the President's second son, should have been at Harvard too, but in 1827 he was expelled and came home to serve as his father's personal secretary. It wasn't a real job, and it certainly left him all the time he needed to flirt and intrigue with Mary, for whom an out-of-sight George was very clearly out of mind. Louisa was frantic, for she could see that this headstrong couple weren't going to wait too long before they consummated their flirtation. For a long time, though, the Presidential head was stuck firmly in the sand. Finally, in February 1828, Louisa got her way and a White House wedding was hastily arranged.

With two injured egos waiting in the wings, it wasn't the happiest of occasions. Though the bridegroom didn't look too elated either, his mother felt. Before taking to her bed, sick at heart, for several days, Louisa found time to write to Charles Francis, reporting that John 'looks already as if he has all the cares of the world on his shoulders'. The bride was unblushingly serene, however, having got what she wanted and turned the First Family upside-down: 'Madame is cool and easy and indifferent as ever,' her new mother-in-law observed.

ANDREW JACKSON, 1829–37

Andrew Jackson wasn't the first or the last politician to have a less than strict regard for truth. Rumours of his birth in a log cabin were greatly exaggerated, for example. Even so, he didn't come from quite the same sort of stock as the WASP elite, whose hold over American political life had been so strong till now. Understandably, Jackson's bitterness had only been increased by the way he'd seen John Quincy Adams apparently 'steal' the 1824 election. Having gone back

Far from being overawed by presidential office, John Quincy Adams looked too comfortable by half, or so his critics felt. They feared the founding of a 'royal' Adams dynasty in the White House.

Andrew Jackson made much of his backwoods background and his down-home manners and ways of thinking, contrasting himself with John Quincy Adams, whose patrician poise had done so much to alienate ordinary American electors.

to Tennessee to lick his wounds, he set himself up at the head of an army of 'Jackson Men' – salt-of-the-earth small farmers, lumberjacks and labourers – determined to wrest power from the new American aristocracy.

To 'Old Hickory', then, belongs the dubious honour of establishing that tradition in American political life in which expensively educated sons of privilege pretend to like nothing better than beer and NASCAR. Jackson set himself up as the Joe Six-Pack of his age. There have been worse crimes in US history, of course. Indeed, Jackson committed one of them himself when, a year into his first term, he signed the Indian Removal Act into US law. The Supreme Court insisted that the Native Americans of the new states beyond the Appalachians had the right to stay where they were, but Jackson overrode their legal judgement, ordering their expulsion from their ancestral homelands in their thousands. The 'little guy' defended so stoutly by Jackson had to be white; likewise, it was liberty for all except for African-Americans – he was dead set against any reform to the laws on slavery. With all his small-d 'democratic' swagger, Jackson didn't have too much time for capital-D democracy: he used his veto more than any previous President.

Defending Rachel's Honour

Andrew Jackson wasn't his First Lady's first husband – that in itself made her a very intriguing figure in a day when respectable women were supposed to be virgin brides. To make matters worse, there was some ambiguity over when they had been legally divorced. This was par for the course at a time when divorce was still quite rare and its ins-and-outs little known or understood – in the new states of the West, moreover,

the law went its own way, and record-keeping could be sketchy. But the upshot was that her marriage to Jackson was believed to have been bigamous.

Thrown out of the house by Robards in 1788, Rachel had gone home to mom and the boarding-house she ran. Divorce proceedings were going through and were uncontested. There's no doubt that she was deeply, madly in love – or that she believed herself a single woman – when she eloped with Andrew Jackson in 1791. Not everyone believed the couple's claims that they'd got married, however. And, even if they had, it became clear that there was at least a technical case for saying that bigamy had been committed, because Rachel and Robards' divorce

'Old Hickory' was indestructible. Not only did he come through 13 duels but, on 30 January, 1835, he survived the first recorded assassination attempt on a US President. His assailant had two pistols but, miraculously, both misfired.

didn't finally come through till 1792. In the end they were reduced to marrying a second time in 1794.

Even now the whispering didn't stop. Jackson, who had a strong sense of pride and a genuine passion for his wife, could be relied upon to fly off the handle at any remark about Rachel's honour. Innumerable brawls resulted, and no fewer than 13 formal duels. One, in 1806, had fatal consequences, the attorney Charles Dickinson wounding the future President before being killed himself. Jackson was lucky to be alive, since Dickinson had narrowly missed his heart: he was so full of bullets, it was said, that he rattled.

MARTIN VAN BUREN, 1837–41

America may be a big country, but politics is a very small world. We should never be surprised at the alliances, enmities and relationships it produces. And, as Europeans haven't been slow to notice, for a nation which set itself up specifically in opposition to the idea of monarchy and inherited rank, America has always had a bit of a weakness for political dynasties. The Adamses we've already seen, but what are we to make of the story that Martin Van Buren was the illegitimate son of Aaron Burr? The evidence is circumstantial at best: Burr was from time to time a guest in the Kinderhook tavern run by Van Buren's parents. Burr was just married himself at the relevant time, and to a wife with whom he was famously head-over-heels in love. But that needn't have stopped him – men compartmentalized, then as now. Burr is known to

> Burr was just married himself at the relevant time, and to a wife with whom he was famously head-over-heels in love. But that needn't have stopped him.

have been attractive to women – does that mean he was irresistible to the tavernkeeper's wife? There's no way of knowing: you pays your money and you takes your choice.

It's true that the 'Fox of Kinderhook' had a masterly cunning and evasive way with words that he could have inherited from the man who may have been his father. Van Buren grew up to have some of Burr's confidence too, his air of assurance and his dandified self-presentation – his taste for fine tailoring was to become controversial as the economy ran into problems, as did the extravagance of his lifestyle more generally. In the end it was as Jackson's 'favourite son'

that Van Buren got the Presidential nomination. He'd served him loyally as Secretary of State and then as Vice President.

The Petticoat President

Rival politicians – and later historians – have pretty much lined up to slight Van Buren and what he achieved in the 'third Jackson Presidency'. It may have been in part a desire to put him down that led to the story that he owed his preferment to his chivalrous behaviour toward Margaret 'Peggy' O'Neale Eaton. The other Cabinet wives would not have anything to do with the better half of the Secretary of War: although she'd married John Eaton as a widow, she was said to have had an affair with him while her first husband had been alive. The 'Petticoat Affair' of 1830–1 sent shockwaves through the Jackson Cabinet, but the President (who had himself suffered at the

Now a National Historic Site, Lindenwald, in the Hudson Valley, was bought by Martin Van Buren during his presidency, though he was not to occupy the 30-room estate until he left the White House in 1841.

Left: Impeccably turned-out as ever, Martin Van Buren ran into some controversy with his taste for fine tailoring and gracious living, at a time when the domestic economy was in difficulties.

hands – or rather the tongues – of the gossips) was firm in his insistence that Peggy should be treated with respect. John Calhoun, till then Jackson's right-hand-man, saw his stock falling: his wife Floride was regarded as the ringleader of the matrons' mutiny; Martin Van Buren reaped the benefit and succeeded him as Vice President.

Human Nature, Human Rights

In 1838, it emerged that Samuel Swartwout, Jackson's appointment as Collector of Customs for the Port of New York, had had his fingers in the till to the tune of almost $2.25 million ($54 million today). Van Buren acted with commendable decision, replacing him with one Jesse Hoyt – only for it to emerge that he too had been on the take. Sadly, such corruption was beginning to lose its capacity to shock Americans, any more than it has a capacity to shock us in the present day. But we're less ready than our forebears were to accept some of the assumptions Van Buren's administration made in what might broadly be labelled 'minorities policy'.

The Eighth President inherited Jackson's policy of Indian Removals, it is true. But he showed no inclination to reverse or even soften it in any way. It was during his term of office that the notorious episode of the 'Trail of Tears' took place. This was

Aaron Burr had notoriously been a ladies' man, but even so the suggestion that Jefferson's Vice President might have been Martin Van Buren's natural father seems far-fetched, even by the standards of political conspiracy theory.

MRS JOHNSON

Van Buren's Vice President, Richard Mentor Johnson, is often said to have scandalized polite society by parading publicly with his 'black mistress', Julia Chinn. All the evidence is, however, that the officially unmarried Johnson regarded her as his common-law wife. She looked after his Kentucky plantation when he was away on business. Julia was still technically a slave and, though light-skinned, officially a 'negro' too, so Johnson couldn't legally

have married her even if he'd wanted to.

An early hero of the Civil Rights movement, then? Well, he was quite capable of using a woman's slave-status against her if it suited him. After Julia's death, Johnson took up with another African-American partner. When she left him for another man, he brought the full weight of the law down upon her. He had her hunted down, arrested and sold at auction.

all about opening up the 'empty' territories of the West for settlement – except, of course, that they weren't really empty but the homes of countless Native American communities. In 1838, 18,000 Cherokee were expelled from territories in Georgia, Tennessee, South Carolina and Alabama. Some 4000 died on the journey to the new home allotted to them in Oklahoma.

The decision to hand back the slaves from *La Amistad* to the ship's Spanish owners could not conceivably be blamed on Jackson, however. The slaves had risen up and seized the vessel the year before. As it sailed north, it had been captured by a US naval ship and brought into port, where the slaves had been kept pending legal hearings to decide upon their fate. Anxious to avoid offending Spain, Martin Van Buren had ordered that the ship and its slaves be handed over, but the judiciary intervened and the slaves were finally freed by the Supreme Court.

WILLIAM HENRY HARRISON, 1841

Blink, and you missed the Presidency of William Henry Harrison, who was only 32 days into his term of office when he died. By way of compensation, he made the longest inaugural address in history: despite cutting by aides, it went on for just under two hours. It was the chill he caught as he stood out in the cold and rain delivering this oration that, graduating to pneumonia in the days that followed, carried Harrison off so soon after.

Battle of Tippecanoe

President Harrison hardly had time to get up to anything untoward. He spent most of his Presidency on what was to be his deathbed. Aged 68, he was in any case perhaps getting a bit too old for mistresses or for hell-raising. Neither does his earlier life afford much satisfaction to the seeker-after-scandal. Today, it's true, we're likely to look askance at the role of 'Old Tippecanoe' as a hero of the wars against Indiana's Native Americans. The nickname came from his victory at the Battle of Tippecanoe.

Harrison's inauguration was the high point of his presidency – indeed it was pretty much the only achievement of his presidential reign. Struck down by sickness, he died just 32 days after taking office.

JOHN TYLER, 1841–5

Harrison's death left America in shock. Even in Washington, where the late-President's ill-health had been more widely known about, no one had expected for a moment that it would end this way – or anything like this soon. There was no real precedent for this situation. Despite general agreement that, as Vice President, John Tyler should take on his chief's responsibilities in a caretaker capacity, few imagined that he would assume the Presidency himself. The obvious man for this job would have been Henry Clay, whom Harrison had narrowly defeated in his bid for the Whig Party (a grouping in favour of modernization and economic protectionism). If not President himself, Clay expected to be the 'power behind the throne'. Abruptly, though, the decision was taken out of his hands.

Self-appointing President

For Tyler had other ideas. It would not be too much of an exaggeration to say that he took the position of President by sheer chutzpah – his actions left Washington as stunned as Harrison's death had done. Before they knew it, President Tyler had delivered his inaugural address. He was de facto President whether

'Old Tippecanoe' was given his nickname because of a battle of 1811, in which the young William Henry Harrison had led US troops to victory over Chief Tecumseh's confederation of Indiana tribes.

anybody liked it or not. There was nothing the two houses of Congress could do but to confirm him in office and sing a rousing chorus of 'Hail to the Chief'.

The modern view that the Vice President is 'a heartbeat away' from the Presidency – the automatic successor when an incumbent dies – is a relatively recent one. It became law only with the ratification of the 25th Amendment in 1967. Tyler's self-appointment was itself, of course, to constitute a precedent of sorts for future Veeps, but we should be in doubt of the audacity of his coup.

Opposition to Tyler didn't disappear, but it had to find alternative angles of attack. Clay, not surprisingly, never forgave him. When the President made use of his veto to frustrate the Whigs' attempts to set up a National Bank as a way of preventing stock-market panics of the sort that had convulsed the economy in 1837, an incandescent Clay led moves to have him expelled from the Whig Party. Tyler went on unperturbed, but his continuing use of the veto raised ever more eyebrows as time went on – it was arguably undemocratic, especially in one who'd never actually been elected President. Eventually ex-President John Quincy Adams called for Tyler's impeachment. In the event, though, Tyler was somehow able to ride out the storm. He very calmly pointed out that the Presidential Veto was explicitly provided for in the Constitution – if as President he had that power, why should he not use it? His enemies had even less success with the charge that he'd acted improperly in paying private individuals to investigate suspected large-scale fraud at the New York Custom House. Was he not to fulfil his constitutional obligation to uphold the law?

Right: John Tyler took presidential power in what amounted to a coup, though in so doing he established the tradition by which the Vice President automatically takes office when an incumbent dies.

Below: New York's Custom House had been a lucrative source of income for corrupt officials. Tyler's critics claimed that he himself had acted constitutionally in trying to bring the guilty men to book.

A NATION DIVIDED

America was growing fast – in population, as immigrants kept on arriving; in geographical extent with the settlement of the West; in economic and political power. Inevitably, it was growing in political complexity as well: with so much more at stake, the struggle for influence was becoming bitter.

◆

'No President who performs his duties faithfully and conscientiously can have any leisure.'

In 1845, there were still men and women alive who could remember when their country had been a scattering of small trading cities and farming communities. Spooked by the scale of a vast and substantially unexplored interior, the Thirteen Colonies had clung to the Atlantic coast. In truth, for all its swagger, the new United States had done the same. The Louisiana Purchase of 1803 had brought

James Polk (left) was ruthlessly competent at a time when the Republic had arguably outgrown the need for idealists. Franklin Pierce (above) was a decent man, but his presidency never really stood a chance.

what we now call the 'Midwest' and 'Deep South' into US hands – at least in theory. But 'ownership' wasn't the same as occupation. As the nineteenth century wore on, the cry went up 'Go west, young man!' and settlers streamed across the Appalachians into the new territories. America was growing rapidly, in every way, but the bigger the country, the greater the scope for political division, it seemed – and the higher the stakes as far as corruption was concerned.

JAMES K. POLK, 1845–9

A great deal of history is 'dark': our leaders have had to be brutally realistic at times even in pursuit of the highest ends (just think of World War II, to pick one very obvious example). Not that our leaders' ends have always been idealistic, by any means – or where would a book like this one be? – but in the real world, good government isn't always pretty. Sometimes, though, the

cynicism of a foreign-policy decision is so brazen it can hardly be ignored; sometimes its effrontery can be nothing short of awe-inspiring.

Such was surely the case when, in 1846, an act of Mexican 'aggression' was used as the justification for the Mexican–American War. US troops had headed south, making a deliberate incursion into Mexican territory and Mexican forces had had the temerity to try to stop them. Such an unprovoked assault could not be tolerated, howled an extremely outraged American press. The next thing anyone knew, the two nations were at war.

There had of course been trouble between them for some years. Since the 1820s, American colonists had been sneaking into what (from the Mexican perspective) was the far-flung border province of *Tejas*; in 1836, with Washington's not-so-quiet encouragement, they'd risen up and proclaimed the independent Republic of Texas. The defence of the Alamo mission had been the ultimate example of how base opportunism could end up being consecrated by the self-sacrificing courage of men and women.

The victory at Buena Vista (1847), which saw the Americans use artillery to overcome a bigger Mexican army, was a triumph not only for James Polk but for his future successor, Zachary Taylor, who commanded US forces in the field that day.

The Mexican–American War was little more than a land-grab – but what a land-grab it was! About half the territory of Mexico! That unfortunate country had until then included not just Texas but much of today's 'American' West and Southwest (Wyoming, Nevada, Utah, Colorado, California and most of Arizona and New Mexico). From a military point of view, if the truth be told, it was like taking candy from a baby: Mexico was in a state of chronic crisis both politically and economically.

A Perfect President?

So, Polk took America to war on cooked-up pretexts: we may see that as a scandal; the people didn't. He had a reputation for making misleading claims in his public statements – so what's new? Or strange? He was a *politician*! The nearest he came to a classic-style scandal came when his administration discreetly

FIGHTING FOR SLAVERY

WHILST IT'S TRUE THAT HIS CONDUCT in bringing on the war doesn't bear close moral scrutiny, Polk would be amazed to see that this adventure has been recorded as some kind of scandal. Neither, for the most part, do today's inhabitants of these western states feel they'd be better off if they still belonged to Mexico.

One thing does stick in the craw for us, though: the fact that Polk seems to have been so strongly motivated by the desire to uphold the right of white landowners to use slave labour. North Carolina-born Polk had inherited over 50 slaves with the family plantation; he remained a slaveowner – and an enthusiastic defender of slavery – all his life. The Texan colonists' main beef with Mexico had been its abolition of slavery in 1821. Since it also created a sanctuary for runaways from the existing states, the move was seen as profoundly destabilizing for the entire South.

Cruelty was inseparable from the institution of slavery in the South: in their desperation, many thousands ran away. Rather than abolish the outrage, America took steps to shut off their sanctuary, a major motive for the Mexican–American War.

channelled $35,000 ($1 million) of government – that is, taxpayers' – money into a Democratic-supporting paper, the *Washington Globe*. Even then, showing an instinctive feel for what a century later would become known as 'deniability', the President made certain he wasn't involved in any of the decisions or shown any of the paperwork. So there you have him: James K. Polk, a statesman to all intents and purposes untouched by scandal. The perfect President? Possibly – though he doesn't come across as especially interesting. A good man? Not many people would agree …

ZACHARY TAYLOR, 1849–50

The American public has always warmed to soldier-statesmen – and not just because they've already demonstrated their principles and their courage in the most demanding of arenas. Typically, too, they seem straightforward, brisk and businesslike, free from the evasiveness that seems ingrained in career-politicians. We've seen it most recently with Colin Powell – tipped in the 1990s as a possible Presidential candidate; we saw it most famously, perhaps, with Eisenhower. There's a case, of course, for arguing that the tradition began with Washington, but, though the 'hero of the hour', he wasn't quite the 'breath of fresh air' his successors were to be. On the one hand, Americans hadn't yet had the chance to grow disillusioned with the normal run of democratic politicians; on the other, there was nothing remotely 'unworldly' about Washington's way with his expenses claims.

'Old Rough and Ready', Zachary Taylor, really was an innocent, though. Born in the aftermath of revolution, in 1788, he'd grown up a soldier, with no apparent interest in politics. He'd served in the War of 1812 and in several patriotic conflicts since, most notably against the Native American peoples in the Black Hawk and Seminole Wars. In February 1847, he'd secured his national hero's status in Saltillo, northern Mexico. There he'd led a small US force to victory against a vast (though also vastly outgunned) Mexican army in what was to be a turning-point in the Mexican–American War.

The victor of Buena Vista, Zachary Taylor was able to convert public adulation into political capital, presenting himself as a career soldier, free of 'baggage' and independent of all vested interests.

Till then, Taylor had been happy to keep his political opinions to himself. He'd never even voted when he became a Presidential candidate in 1848, when he was 62. (He'd never been in one place long enough to register.) 'I have no private purposes to accomplish,' he wrote to a friend, explaining his decision, 'no party projects to build up, no enemies to punish – nothing to serve but my country.' The issue which first galvanized him into taking a stand was that of the need for sound finance: he'd been outraged when Andrew Jackson let the Second Bank of the United States collapse 12 years before.

Paradoxically, Taylor's naivety was his making as a politician. He was direct in style, but he managed to be evasive none the less. A slaveowner, he didn't favour the extension of slavery into the western states – though this was on pragmatic rather than on moral grounds as many in the North assumed. While his support for states' rights won him support in the South, where a secessionist mood was already growing,

> 'Old Rough and Ready', Zachary Taylor really was an innocent, though. Born in the aftermath of revolution, in 1788, he'd grown up a soldier, with no apparent interest in politics.

his insistence that Americans should stand together went down much better in the North. Without deliberately setting out to deceive, he managed to be all things to all voters. Most of all, of course, he was the people's hero.

The Galphin Claim

If President Taylor was so old and unworldly he seemed to be a relic of another age, what are we to make of the single major scandal that sullied his Presidency? The claim by the Galphin family of Georgia to a sum of $43,500 ($1.3 million today) dated all the way back to the days of British rule. Their ancestor, George Galphin, a trader, had claimed the sum as being owed to him by the Creek and Cherokee peoples; the British had agreed to pay him this money

So clear was Zachary Taylor's advantage in the fight for the White House as the 1848 election approached that a cartoonist proclaimed him 'Cock of the Walk' before the polls had even had a chance to open.

out of the proceeds gained from selling lands these peoples had given up to them. The Revolutionary War had come and gone and Georgia's Native peoples expelled from their old homes, but the Galphin family still wanted what it was owed. Many people will be surprised to learn that, in 1848, the US Government eventually acknowledged – and, more to the point, paid – this debt.

It wasn't enough for the family, or for their attorney George W. Crawford, who agreed to battle on for 73 years' worth of interest – on the basis that he would receive 50 per cent if it was paid. When Crawford was taken on by Taylor as Secretary of War, the conflict of interest could hardly have been clearer. He got his Cabinet colleague, the Treasury Secretary William Meredith, to pass the payment – but no matter, the official responsible refused the claim. Crawford now

went way beyond any remotely acceptable limits by pressing Meredith to try again. The Treasury Secretary this time simply overrode his comptroller, the Galphins got their interest and Crawford his 'cut' of $100,000 ($2.9 million today).

Sadly, but inevitably, President Taylor was badly damaged when the news got out. Whilst no one imagined for a moment that he had been aware of what his subordinates were up to, the affair called into question both his competence and his judgement. His old age and his innocence became sticks to beat him with: all of a sudden, he seemed doddery and out of touch.

A Presidential Poisoning?

Aged he may have been, but Zachary Taylor appeared to be in perfect health when, at a public event on Independence Day, 1850, he is said to have sat down to a snack of cherries in cold milk. He was almost certainly offered other snacks by members of the public in the hours that followed but was soon unable to eat anything, being seriously ill, apparently struck

> It didn't help that the official record of where the President had been, what he'd done and even what he'd eaten that day was very sketchy – no one had expected that these things would ever matter.

down by gastroenteritis. By 8 July he was dead: it had all been so sudden that speculation was inevitable. It didn't help that the official record of where the President had been, what he'd done and even what he'd eaten that day was very sketchy – no one had expected that these things would ever matter. The rumours wouldn't go away, and in 1991 his body was actually exhumed so tests could be carried out for arsenic. We now know for certain that Zachary Taylor *wasn't* poisoned – or not, at least, with arsenic; most

likely, some of the milk he had was bad. But wherever an important death is unexplained, conspiracy theories flourish: they continue unabated to this day.

MILLARD FILLMORE, 1850–3

After Taylor's sudden death in 1850, his Vice President was hastily sworn in as his successor. Millard Fillmore is among the duller figures to hold the Presidency. From the point of view of posterity (and of the Northern abolitionists of his own day), his zealous support for his predecessor's Fugitive Slave Act was a scandal: this reaffirmed the rights of slaveowners to have escapees hunted down and penalized those public officials who refused to help them on conscientious grounds. A scandal indeed: does it make it better or

Forever associated with Millard Fillmore, the Fugitive Slave Act of 1850 made the apprehension of escaped slaves a matter of public 'duty'. Officials deemed to have assisted escapees, actively or passively, were punishable by law.

Millard Fillmore must be a contender for the title of America's most boring president. His main claim to fame is that he installed the first bathtub in the White House. And amusingly that story isn't even true!

worse that Fillmore wasn't personally some foam-flecked racist but a cold-fish administrator out for nothing more than a quiet life? 'God knows but I detest slavery,' he wrote in a letter to a friend, 'but it is an existing evil … and we must endure it and give it such protection as is guaranteed by the Constitution.'

A Tale of a Tub

It somehow had to be Fillmore for whom the humorist H.L. Mencken came up with his 'Bathtub Hoax': with any other President, there'd have been some actual incident, some real colour to distract us from the joke … In 1917, out of sheer mischief, Mencken published an article in the *New York Evening Mail* purporting to be a history of the bathtub. It had been introduced to America as recently as 1850, Mencken claimed, but had met with much resistance from a population firmly wedded to its filth. They were discouraged too by dire warnings from their doctors about the dangers of bathing – which promoted all manner of rheumatic and other ills, they said. It had taken the statesmanlike intervention of the President to change attitudes: Fillmore had installed the first bathtub in the White House.

Jane Pierce was never able to recover from the tragic loss of her third son Bennie (shown with Jane here) in a railroad accident, an event which derailed her husband's presidency before it had even begun.

A particularly handsome specimen, lined with lead and with a carved mahogany surround.

The rest was history … Of course, it wasn't really – though Mencken's did become one of the all-time historic hoaxes. He himself lived long enough to look back in (slightly puzzled) pride and wonder, in 1949, at how completely and uncritically his story had been accepted, and 'not as foolishness but as fact, and not only in newspapers but in official documents and other works of the highest pretensions'. Long before the age of the Internet, it's clear, nonsensical whimsy was being accepted as history, often passed on by researchers who really should have known better.

FRANKLIN PIERCE, 1853–7

The general historical consensus has been that 'Handsome Frank' was a failure as US President – not bad or stupid, but a decent guy out of his depth. And these were definitely deep waters. For decades, the supposedly 'United' States had been split by the row over slaveholding and states' rights in what we can now see was a slow and difficult descent into civil war. Both Taylor and Fillmore had found themselves forced into painful contortions to try and satisfy both sides. But Pierce, a compromise candidate to begin with, was pretty much a broken man before he even took his inauguration oath.

Easy-going and mild-mannered by statesman's standards, he was a cheerful and sociable character, and an accomplished speaker, but he had a shyer side. And he'd married a strikingly timid wife, Jane Appleton Pierce, who'd never really been happy with her husband's participation in public life. (Had never, gossips muttered, been

CUT-PRICE CUBA

IN 1854, MEMBERS OF PIERCE'S administration attempted to come up with a plan for buying Cuba – then a colonial possession of the Spanish. They were going to offer $110 million – a snip for an island worth much more for its tobacco plantations alone, leaving aside its strategic significance in the Caribbean. If Madrid didn't prove cooperative, the plan was to plead slave unrest as a pretext for intervening and taking the island by force. In the event, their cover was blown when abolitionist supporters got wind of the plan and feared that Cuba was destined to be admitted to the Union and would tip the political balance as another slaveowning state. The resulting press furore painted Pierce as a swashbuckling brigand, which was quite unfair – even if the plan had been put into execution, it would hardly have been more piratical than Polk's attack on Mexico less than 10 years before.

Its sugar and cigars made Cuba an attractive possession, but its strategic importance was also immense – while its admission to the Union would have bolstered the strength of the slaveholding states.

happy with her husband, full stop.) They didn't seem the most obvious choice for an American 'First Couple'.

Both would appear to have been borderline-depressed: two of their three sons had died in early childhood; the third, Benjamin, or 'Bennie', was killed right before their eyes. Passengers together in a train which had left the tracks and tumbled down an embankment at Andover, Massachusetts, they'd been forced to look on as he'd been crushed to death. And it all happened just two months before Franklin Pierce's swearing-in, so there was no time or space to recover or even satisfactorily to mourn a loss that would have laid far stronger couples low.

Drink Takes Over

Between the shock of bereavement and of her unwanted elevation to the First Lady's role, Jane pretty much gave up the struggle. The 'Shadow of the White House' withdrew almost completely from public life. Franklin kept things together – after some fashion – with the help of copious quantities of alcohol. This only increased the gulf further between him and Jane, who not only didn't drink herself but took a seriously dim view of drinking as signed-up member of the Temperance Movement. For all the sympathy people felt, moreover, it also made the President something of a laughing-stock in Washington, where it was noticed that no one ever seemed to see him sober. There was no nuclear trigger in those days, but even so the Presidency was supposed to be a sufficiently demanding role that it couldn't successfully be discharged by someone who was three sheets to the wind. It was no great surprise, therefore, when Pierce consequently failed to secure his nomination for a second term – or when his cheerful reaction was: 'There's nothing left … but to get drunk.'

JAMES BUCHANAN, 1857–61

Viewed in strictly historical terms, the chief 'scandal' of Buchanan's reign was his failure to bind the running sore that was Southern secessionism. Like his predecessors, he stood (and often stands) accused of giving too much away in his desperation to keep the Union intact. But Buchanan's Presidency was also at fault for the handing-out of government contracts in return for campaign contributions – traditional graft, but on an unprecedented scale. Printing contracts were especially lavish: friends of the administration were handed exorbitant sums for minor jobs: they were effectively being given a license to print money.

Buchanan himself seems to have been a fairly passive participant in such shenanigans – though it might well be asked what business does a President have *being* passive. (And what justification could there conceivably be for his shabby treatment of the House Committee led by 'Honest' John Covode? Its legitimate criticisms were dismissed as an unpatriotic attack on the integrity of the US Presidency.) The most extravagant deals seem to have been done by his Secretary of War, John B. Floyd – though even he appears to have been a weak and over-obliging man rather than an outright thief. Just a Secretary who couldn't say no, it seems, he bought pockets of land from supporters on the government's behalf for outrageous sums and sold bonds on military purchasing contracts that did not yet even exist. Yet he was persistent,

As Buchanan's Secretary of War, John B. Floyd proved incorrigibly corrupt, though he was at the same time oddly innocent – he never seems to have fully understood the implications of the dirty deals he did.

> For all the sympathy people felt, moreover, it also made the President something of a laughing-stock in Washington, where it was noticed that no one ever seemed to see him sober.

for all his passivity. When an embarrassed Buchanan did attempt to rein him in, he carried on regardless, till finally persuaded to quit his post: even then he had the face to claim he was resigning on a matter of principle.

Oh don't! Governor Pickens, don't fire! till I get out of office.

We are, however, ignoring what might be called the elephant in Buchanan's Oval Office: the major question marks over his sexuality. The only President never to have married, Buchanan had briefly been engaged at the outset of his career, in 1819, but his fiancée had broken off their engagement and died soon after. There was some suspicion that the young woman – a rich industrialist's daughter, Ann Caroline Coleman – might have committed suicide. Her doctor believed she had taken an overdose of laudanum (a

---

The aged Andrew Jackson referred to Rufus as 'Miss Nancy'; for others he was 'Miss Fancy'.

---

mix of opium and wine, then popular as an aid to sleep). Buchanan swore that he would never marry but remain faithful to her memory. A noble self-sacrifice – or did it suit him down to the ground?

For, while Buchanan continued to enjoy easy (and frequently flirtatious) relationships with women in Washington's social whirl, there was never any sign that he was drawn to a more intimate involvement. When he did set up house, indeed, it was with another man, William Rufus King, the Senator for Alabama and subsequently President Pro Tempore of the US Senate. An odd but clearly devoted couple, they shared a house for 15 years, separating only when Buchanan moved into the White House as President (Buchanan brought his niece, Harriet Lane, to do the hosting duties of First Lady). Contemporaries were in little doubt of the nature of their relationship: the aged Andrew Jackson referred to Rufus as 'Miss Nancy'; for others he was 'Miss Fancy'; whilst Buchanan's Postmaster General, Aaron V. Brown, spoke to friends of 'Buchanan and his wife'. Far from resenting such gibes, the President seems to have revelled in them. When Rufus had to go to France on official business, Buchanan complained of his loneliness, writing in one letter: 'I am now solitary and alone, having no companion in the house. I have

'I'll be blowed if I don't fire,' says South Carolina's secessionist Governor Francis Pickens to President Buchanan, standing in front of the cannon he's about to set off in this cartoon of 1861.

JAMES BUCHANAN,
DEMOCRATIC CANDIDATE FOR FIFTEENTH PRESIDENT OF THE UNITED STATES.

Buchanan's contemporaries certainly speculated about his private life. From our perspective, however, the curious thing is how incurious – beyond a certain point – they were; how easy they found it to respect their President's privacy.

gone a wooing to several gentlemen, but have not succeeded with any of them …'

Was America's 15th President 'gay'? It depends on who you ask; and we'll never know for certain. The sleeping arrangements through the years when he and Rufus were roommates weren't divulged. Historians warn against reading too much into their relationship: bachelorhood was in no sense abnormal, they say; men often expressed much more emotion around each other than has since become customary; they were much more demonstrative with one another than they are now. Sure, reply the radical gay scholars: homosexuality was widespread in nineteenth-century America; a great many men – some of them in positions of great importance and authority – were homosexual. In what was still a comparatively deferential age, the public didn't necessarily expect to sit in judgement on the private conduct of its political elite; didn't expect to see its dirty linen in the daily press. The result was that 'open secrets' of this sort were easily tolerated. It was nobody else's business to rock the boat.

On the Slide

It wasn't as if people didn't have other things to worry about. America gave every impression of being on a slippery slope toward disintegration. The tensions that had for a decade or more been pulling its Presidents this way and that, appeared at last to be reaching some sort of breaking-point. How far Buchanan was to blame for South Carolina's secession and the Civil War that followed is hard to say. The same charge had been

levelled against all the Presidents in this chapter: they'd failed to hold together a Union which seemed destined to bust apart. Buchanan's power to influence events was in any case becoming tenuous – he was practically a spectator at his own Democratic Party Convention in 1860. His party colleagues were themselves split down the middle, and no match electorally for the Republicans. They had not only an extraordinarily inspirational leader in Abraham Lincoln but a vital weapon in the Report of the Covode Committee.

Just good friend or partner? William Rufus King lived with James Buchanan for fifteen years. They were deridingly referred to as 'Buchanan and his wife', but might that actually have been how they saw themselves?

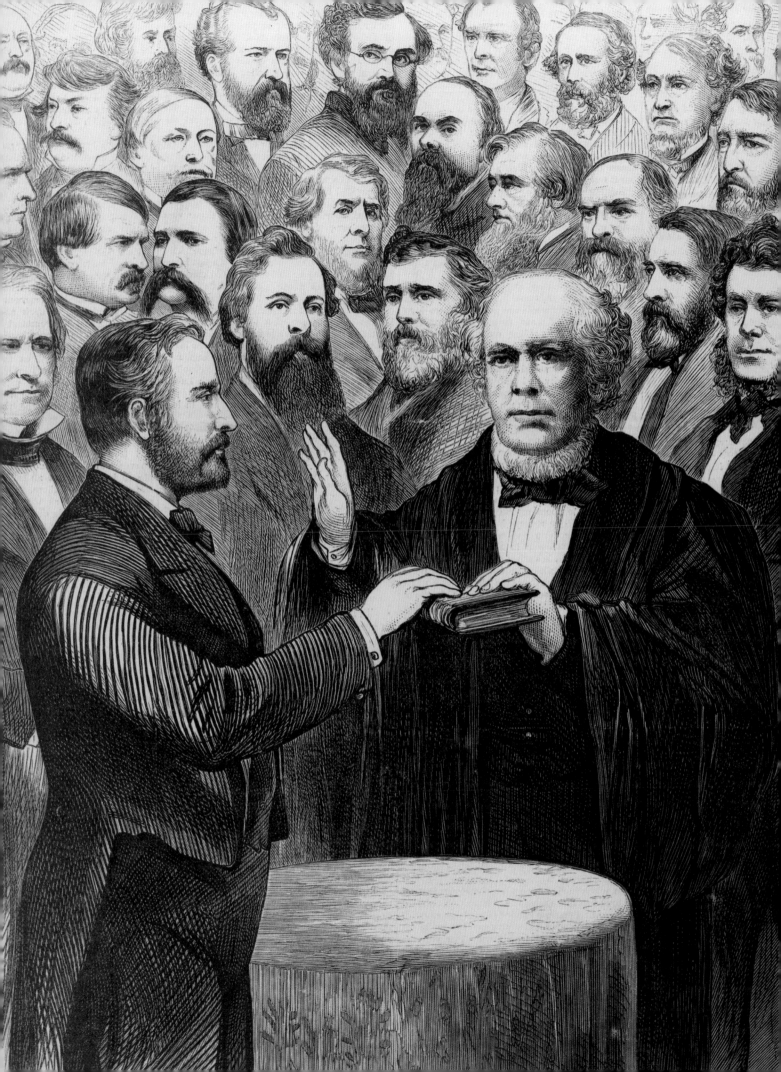

IV

CIVIL WAR AND RECONSTRUCTION

The nation's darkest hour – and the dawning of a new era – the Civil War was a pivotal point in US history. The scandals went on, however: America's emergency was the crooks' opportunity, reconstruction a license for sharps and swindlers to print money.

'If I were two-faced, would I be wearing this one?'

The American Civil War broke out on 12 April 1861. The conflict tore the United States apart. Often described as the 'first modern war', it didn't just 'turn brother against brother' but armed them with industrially produced ordnance and rapid-fire weapons. Well over half a million lives were lost; countless more men and women were left maimed and crippled; communities were traumatized. It was a national tragedy, in which the usual political skulduggery was overshadowed. But that did not mean

Ulysses S. Grant showed impressive presidential presence at his inauguration (left), but after that it was downhill all the way. Even Abraham Lincoln (above) was slower than he should have been to stop corruption.

that there'd been some sort of suspension of human nature: behind the drumbeat of battle, corrupt routines went on – were redoubled, indeed.

War is a godsend to graft: there isn't the leisure for decisions to be scrutinized. Huge orders have to be made – for horses, feed, rations, weapons, ammunition, knapsacks … you name it – and then continually renewed. Massive contracts are scattered like confetti: who's going to notice a bit of padding here and there? But desperate times also bring outrageous larcenies: many of the procurement deals agreed at this time were much more padding than substance. Historian Thomas A. Bailey points to one agreement by which three western forts were built at an enormouse price of $191,000 ($4.8 million today) – three times more than the work can have conceivably cost – and a Boston purchasing agent who raked in a commission of $20,000 ($502,000 today) in a single week.

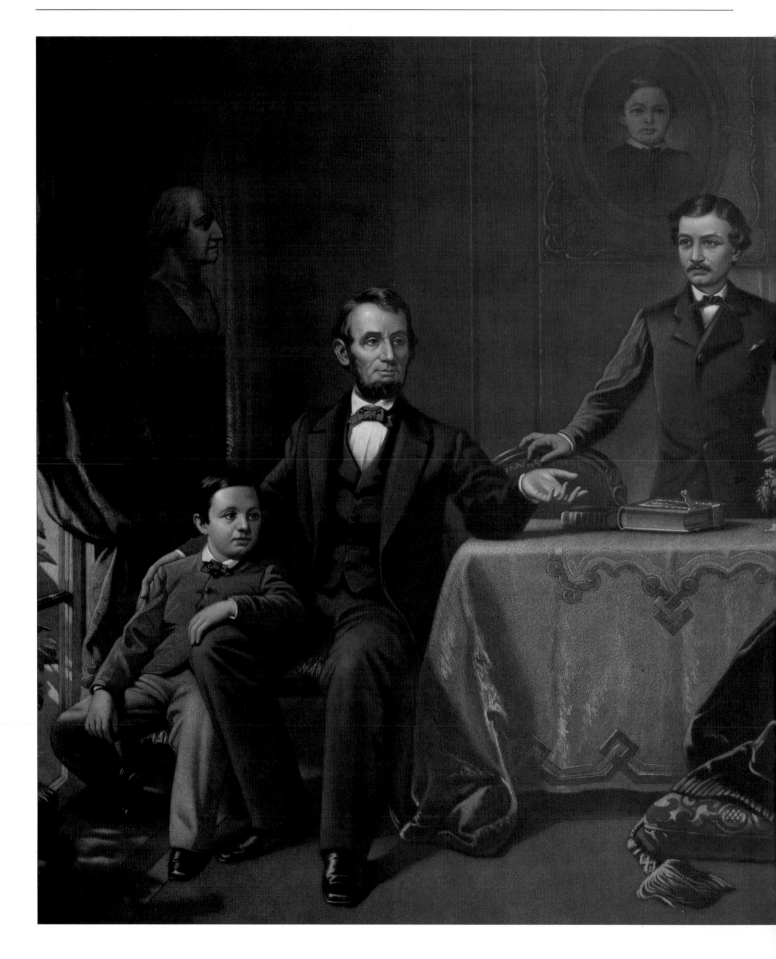

ABRAHAM LINCOLN, 1861–5

Lincoln wasn't so much a President as a 'tyrant', his opponents charged. The advocate of 'government of the people, by the people, for the people' had turned democracy into dictatorship. And it's difficult to deny it. One of Lincoln's first acts on taking office was the suspension of *Habeas Corpus* – an 'inalienable right' under English law since Anglo-Saxon times. The Latin name means 'you shall have the body', and it literally means that, when the state arrests someone, they have to put up or shut up promptly – charge him or her within a short space of time or set them free. Now, though, Lincoln's government could round up suspected 'Copperheads' – Confederate sympathizers in the Northern states – and intern them indefinitely, without charge or trial. Apparently embarrassed, the President introduced special military courts which allowed at least the appearance of some form of 'due process' to take place. But, as with the tribunals held a century and a half later to 'try' the Guantanamo inmates, these courts were conducted in strict secrecy, the 'evidence' invoked never revealed.

God's gift to democracy also took measures to have the electoral polls in crucial swing-states 'supervised': while rough-looking, well-armed heavies from the Lincoln Republican side looked on, voters had to file past carrying coloured cards that showed the way they planned to vote. Southern-supporting newspapers were shut down; their editors arrested. As is always the case, it wasn't just those who were directly affected who were silenced. Lincoln's government created a climate of real fear.

Secretary of Sleaze

On 11 January 1862, the President wrote to Simon Cameron, expressing 'my confidence in your ability, patriotism, and fidelity to public trust'. The Secretary of War had been not-so-gently pressured to resign and was indeed being sent to the diplomatic doghouse as US Ambassador to Russia, so it can't have cost Lincoln much to find a few kind words. Even so, it's a surprisingly glowing reference for one who'd brought

The Lincoln family presents a united front, but this was to some extent a White House divided: it cost Mary dearly to make the stand she did against her southern homeland and Confederate kin.

such disgrace upon himself and the administration he served: corruption had been rife under his stewardship. There's a case for saying that this has to be among the most dishonest statements 'Honest Abe' ever made, though some historians point to a larger pattern.

Despite abundant evidence that Cameron's office was haemorrhaging cash in a time of crisis, Lincoln had been strikingly loath to act. This most self-assured and even arrogant of men had to be pushed into taking action by colleagues and officials; and he went out on a limb to defend him after he'd gone.

There's no reason whatsoever to think that Lincoln was corrupt himself, but he was by any standards a complex man, and the suggestion has been made that he was at some level drawn to the gamier side of his Secretary of War. Cameron was a charmer; he was also what the British call a 'chancer' – an instinctive opportunist; his cavalier dash and easy-going lack of scruple were intriguing to a straight-up, belt-and-braces type like Lincoln.

The Great Procrastinator

The Great Emancipator? Well, yes and no. Lincoln dragged his feet about freeing the Confederacy's slaves – partly because he felt it would be a meaningless gesture before he could actually enforce this law. Those slaves who gained their freedom in the early stages of the Civil War did so by themselves – basically, by running away and heading for the North – though they undoubtedly felt encouraged by the Confederacy's unfolding crisis. That the President had long and sincerely sought the liberation of the slaves is not in serious doubt, but there was still a generous dash of mischief-making in his

> This most self-assured and even arrogant of men had to be pushed into taking action by colleagues and officials; and he went out on a limb to defend him after he'd gone.

Emancipation Proclamation. He issued it in 1862, in the aftermath of the Battle of Antietam, from which the Union's forces had emerged victorious but distinctly bruised. Lincoln seems to have played the liberation card at this point because he sensed that things weren't going entirely his way; he had to make things harder for the South. As far as it went, the tactic worked: local uprisings took place across the Confederacy, whose economy was badly hit; and over 200,000 ex-slaves joined up under the banner of the North.

The Southern Spiritualist

The First Lady's lot is never an easy one, despite the obvious privileges of the position. At a time of civil war, it is that much harder. Especially when the nation's capital sits on the faultline between two opposing blocs – indeed, practically on the frontline in their conflict, and the President's wife has

A passionate and also complex individual to begin with, Mary Lincoln suffered the loss of loved ones on both sides in the Civil War. She was, of course, to lose her husband in the hour of victory.

loyalties on both sides. A child of Lexington, Kentucky, Mary Todd Lincoln was close to her husband, and his staunch supporter, but she had strong connections of family and friendship in the other camp. Some were killed, and Mary inevitably found it hard to do justice to either her own grief or that of her kith and kin in the Confederacy. Especially when she and her husband were already mourning the death of their third son William Wallace, or 'Willie' – he'd sickened and died of typhus on the eve of the Civil War. Since their second son, Eddie, had also died – just before Willie's birth 11 years before – she was pretty much stunned by bereavement even before the shooting even started. It seems to have been at this time that she first became involved in Spiritualism, attempting to contact the spirits of the dead – there

Quite literally crazed by grief, perhaps, Mary Lincoln became increasingly eccentric in the years of her widowhood. Obsessively anxious about money, the former First Lady held sales to auction off her old clothes.

are claims that Abraham too was present for at least some of these White House séances.

The trauma of war proved far too much, and Mary slumped into a deep depression, afflicted by headaches that went on for days. (These seem to have been psychosomatic in origin, though it can't have helped when she sustained a severe blow to the head when her carriage crashed. This incident appears to have been an early assassination attempt aimed at her husband, although he wasn't actually with Mary at the time.) Along with her depression went (occasionally violent) mood-swings: on several occasions she rowed with the President in public. In the circumstances, a spot of retail therapy doesn't seem too bad an idea, though Mary did attract some criticism for her spending on the White House. With a particular taste for fancy drapery, she managed to go $6000 ($132,000 today) over budget.

She'd already suffered more than her fair share of bereavement by the time her beloved husband was assassinated in 1865. Six years later her youngest son, Thomas 'Tad' Lincoln, died. Almost literally maddened by grief, she attempted suicide several times. In between these bouts of despair, in her determination to have her husband's contribution to

ABE'S OTHER LOVES?

LINCOLN HAD MET SPRINGFIELD storekeeper Joshua Fry Speed as a young lawyer in 1837, and the future President roomed with him in the apartment he had above his store. The two became firm friends, and when he came to office Lincoln tried to persuade his friend to take a post in his administration, though Speed preferred to maintain a more background role. A few years ago, the claim was made that letters had been found which proved that the two men had been lovers, but this evidence (if that was what it was) has yet to be produced. Too much really shouldn't be read into reports that Lincoln and Speed said fulsome things about their 'love' for one another: men weren't yet from Mars, and expressed themselves very differently at that time. Neither, though, should we raise our eyebrows to learn that they shared beds during campaign-stops. America was still a frontier society; accommodation was short; and people took a very matter-of-fact view of this sort of thing.

The same health-warnings have to be heeded with regard to the stories about Lincoln and his 'Bucktail soldier'. But the President's relationship with Captain David Derickson was close enough to cause comment at the time. The Captain, who served as the President's bodyguard between 1862 and 1863, was said by one aide's wife to be 'devoted' to his master, and to share a bed with him whenever Mrs Lincoln was out of town.

Billy Greene, who went back even farther with Lincoln than Joshua Speed had done, recalled sharing a bed back in the day in Salem, when both had been in their twenties. In fairness, the future President may have been oblivious of the fact that (in Greene's words) 'his thighs were as perfect as a human being could be', but it does suggest that such co-sleeping arrangements weren't necessarily completely innocent on both sides.

Joshua Fry Speed had been a good and close friend of Lincoln's since his days as a young lawyer in Illinois. Some scholars believe that the two men were lovers: they were certainly very close.

Lincoln's assassin, John Wilkes Booth, was no outcast or loser but one of his country's most successful actors. But he was also a sworn defender of the South and its ideals.

the country fully recognized, she launched a long and sometimes unseemly campaign to secure what she saw as her pension rights. At once wildly extravagant and flamboyantly miserly, she became terrified that 'they' would take her fortune away, and she notoriously went about with $56,000 ($1 million today) in Treasury Bonds sewn inside her petticoats.

Like so many in that era she became obsessed with the desire to communicate with those who had 'gone before' and became ever more deeply involved in the Spiritualist movement.

ANDREW JOHNSON, 1865–9

Lincoln's successor was a statesman of a kind it's hard for us to admire, let alone to like. He was an unapologetic racist who became positively indignant about what he saw as attempts to place African-Americans on an equal footing. His adoption as Lincoln's running-mate had been down to his unusual status as a Union-supporting Southerner. It had never been the intention that he should ever actually be President, of course – assassination hadn't been part of Lincoln's plan. Johnson had been genuinely outraged at the South's secession. Brought up in poverty after his father died, Johnson had developed a consuming hatred of the ruling planter

class – but in other respects he was also very much a product of their society. 'Damn the negroes,' he had cursed as his country spiralled into conflict in 1861: 'I am fighting those traitorous aristocrats, their masters.'

Lack of Schooling

His views on African-Americans had been spelled out in unlovely detail over the years in a series of speeches. 'If you liberate the negro,' he'd asked rhetorically in 1844, 'what will be the next step?' His answer?

The master–slave relationship, he'd said in 1857, was the only appropriate one between whites and 'an inferior type of man … incapable of advancement in his native country'. Johnson had never received any sort of schooling, and he deserves credit for teaching

> Brought up in poverty after his father died, Johnson had developed a consuming hatred of the ruling planter class – but in other respects he was very much a product of their society.

himself to read and write when he was 17, but he became the type of bigot who wears his ignorance with pride. In the circumstances, his hatred for the do-gooding Yankee elite may seem understandable, but his contempt for his black countrymen seems hard to pardon now.

When the fighting was finished, and the Union safely restored, he quickly reverted to Southern type. He leaned over backwards to accommodate the white-ruled former-Confederacy. Northern Republicans felt he was far too quick to decide that the Southern states had done enough to reform and that bygones should be bygones – though, in fairness, Lincoln had favoured leniency as well. In 1866, however, Johnson went too far in Republican eyes when he used his Presidential veto to block civil rights for the former slaves. The 'Black Codes' his appointees brought in instead confirmed African-Americans in their second-class status: they weren't entitled even to aspire to equality – this was now the law. Johnson also blocked attempts to provide federal aid for freed slaves who'd been left in destitution.

Left: Andrew Johnson strikes his most statesmanlike pose, a portrait of George Washington beside him on the table. Johnson presented himself as inheritor of his legacy, a unifying leader for the aftermath of war.

Below: 'Black Codes' ensured that African Americans secured only the most theoretical form of freedom. They were not allowed to own land, vote or refuse to do any work when required by local landowners.

Reconstruction and its Discontents

The word 'Reconstruction' referred to different things. How far the South had to rebuild itself politically and administratively was open to debate – indeed President Johnson felt able to declare Reconstruction officially accomplished within a few months of the war's end in 1865. The slaves had been freed; new state governors appointed … what more could anyone want? Northern Republicans in Congress weren't impressed and, with Johnson now virtually at war with his supposed support in the Capitol, they created their own new state administrations, composed of Northern 'carpetbaggers' and Southern Unionist 'Scalawags'. Neither species was conspicuous by either its moral principles or its financial probity, and with huge

> Too stubborn to give ground, he'd become more or less completely detached from the ongoing political process: his obstinacy had the net effect of weakness. Johnson tried to rebuild his position in 1866 by making a 'Swing Around the Circle'.

funds for redevelopment sloshing around (railroads, highways, schools …), the opportunities for graft were limitless. Granted, the corruption charge was an easy one for disgruntled Southerners to hurl, but few historians have any illusions about the resulting free-for-all.

The President himself doesn't seem to have been anything more than a bystander. After all, this 'Second Reconstruction' hadn't been his idea. To that extent, he's absolved by history. But in a sense he oversaw all these goings-on: the very least that can be said is that they happened on his Presidential watch. Too stubborn to give ground, he'd become

Thaddeus Stevens brings the Johnson impeachment proceedings to a close: a key mover in the President's prosecution, Stevens had been so indefatigable that he'd had himself carried into the chamber when he was seriously ill.

BLAMING THE JEWS

IT WOULD BE NICE TO THINK that Grant was drunk when he composed his notorious General Order 11, though it seems unlikely. It was issued in November 1862, at the height of the Vicksburg Campaign.

All Jews were to be expelled from the area controlled by the Tennessee Military Department, it decreed. Its 'justification' was that the Union war effort in the region was being undermined by the activities of black-marketeers. In time-honoured fashion, Grant blamed Jewish traders. Lincoln later countermanded the order; and Grant himself backtracked when it came to his Presidential campaign of 1868. Was Grant anti-Semitic? Well, obviously, the Order speaks for itself; at the same time, though, he had genuine and enduring friendships with individual Jews. Some of these long predated his political career, so can't easily be put down to opportunism. Such friends included the financiers Jesse and Joseph Seligman, the latter of whom was Grant's first choice as Treasury Secretary, though for personal reasons he felt unable to take up the post.

more or less completely detached from the ongoing political process: his obstinacy had the net effect of weakness. Johnson tried to rebuild his position in 1866 by making a 'Swing Around the Circle', a speaking tour taking in key Northern cities. This was a more radical measure than it may sound: it wasn't yet customary for even candidates to make these campaigning sweeps; still less did this 'circus' seem appropriate for a sitting President. It rebounded on Johnson in the worst possible way: he was drunk at some appearances, some said (we don't know how justly); his inflammatory rhetoric did nothing to appease the Northern crowds; and that he flew off the handle with hecklers robbed the President of yet more dignity.

Impeachment

Johnson tried to shore up his authority by sacking Secretary of War Edwin M. Stanton, replacing him with the more tractable General Lorenzo Thomas. Congress overruled his decision, though, and when Johnson overruled their overruling, Stanton sat tight, literally barricading himself in his office. There had been calls for John Tyler's impeachment (see p64–65), but proceedings against President Johnson were actually begun. And very nearly concluded, indeed, Johnson eventually being acquitted only by a single vote. There were persistent reports that several senators had been bribed by offers of money or influential jobs.

ULYSSES S. GRANT, 1869–77

No one had done more to win the Civil War for the Union than General Ulysses S. Grant; nor to drive home the victory of justice in the South. It was he who, in the Reconstruction era, led the US Army in its campaigns to uphold the rights of African-Americans and destroy the Ku Klux Klan. No wonder, then, that he should have been such a hero in the North, or that he should be swept triumphantly to office in the elections of 1868. Unfortunately, his record as President was to be as dismal as his military service had been illustrious: corruption was regrettably the order of the day.

Oddly enough, though, Grant hadn't particularly impressed even as a soldier at first. He'd graduated from West Point, but only around the middle of his year. There'd been nothing wrong with his record in the Mexican–American War, but his career had then stagnated. In an isolated post out West, he'd developed a drinking problem. This became so severe that, in 1854, he had to resign to avoid a court martial. He ended up back home, helping out in his father's leather store. There he would have remained had it not been for the outbreak of Civil War seven years later. The Union Army couldn't be quite so choosy

The Civil War had seen Ulysses S. Grant at his best. But, sadly, the strong soldier made a weak and ineffective president, all too easily manipulated by the corrupt cronies he collected about himself.

now. Enlisting as a Colonel, he proved himself in action and quickly moved up the hierarchy to become General.

He was still walking something of a tightrope, though, because in between triumphs in the field he'd lose days (and dignity) to drinking bouts – something of which his superiors took a dim view. He'd also acquired himself another unhealthy habit, smoking his way through anything up to 20 cigars a day. The sight of him calmly chomping on his cigar as battle raged about him was immensely reassuring to his men, however, and in later life the cigar became a sort of trademark. For now, it seemed to be talismanic: Grant continued to rack up impressive victories and by 1864 he'd been appointed General-in-Chief. Even now, alcohol was a problem. Despite the presence of future-First Lady Julia on campaign – to keep him in line, it was said – he was regularly and outrageously drunk.

Grant's administration was only eight months old when it was hit by the first of a series of scandals, though the Fisk/Gould Scandal had nothing to do with government corruption in the normal sense. Pure private enterprise on the part of two financiers, James Fisk and Jay Gould, it was an ingenious scheme, founded on the fact that the government had issued huge quantities of banknotes without adequate gold reserves to back them up. It had been an emergency

measure, and almost certainly justified in the circumstances of the Civil War, but now peace had been restored, the government would have to buy them back. It occurred to Fisk and Gould that, if they could corner the gold market, they would be able to name their price.

It was vital to the success of their scheme that the government should not itself start selling gold, so Grant's brother-in-law Abel Corbin was brought on side. He was able to secure them access so they could lobby against the idea of selling gold, and even to persuade the President to appoint an Assistant Treasurer of their choice. General Daniel Butterfield had already agreed to keep on making the case against selling, and to tip the conspirators off if the policy changed. As Gould started buying up gold, Grant – no fool – saw what was happening. He gave the order

> Grant's easy-going management style seems to have been read as an open invitiation to corruption by a host of unscrupulous officials both within and outside his administration.

to sell, and the gold market collapsed. This prompted a more general stock-market panic. Gould and Fisk were warned in time, though, and it is ironic that Abel Corbin was ruined while Grant's own reputation sustained a severe blow.

Grant and Graft

Grant's easy-going management style seems to have been read as an open invitation to corruption by a host of unscrupulous officials both within and outside his administration. The Emma Silver Mine was a case in point: the Utah mine was long since exhausted, but swindlers hoped to sell it to gullible investors in Great Britain. A conventional fraud – except that the

Sherman's March to the Sea (1864) had taken the fight to the South itself, ravaging territories far behind the Confederate front line. Such actions shortened the Civil War, but left a lasting legacy of resentment.

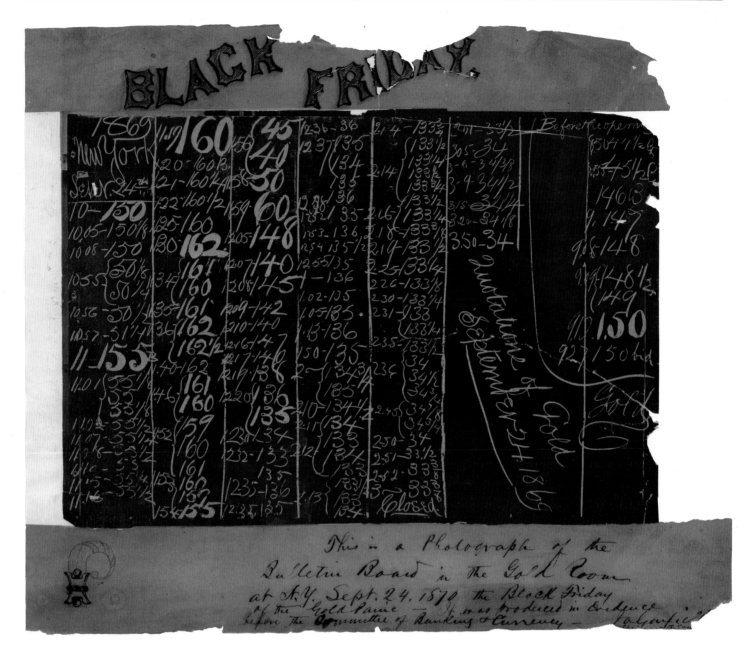

The figures tell the story, tracing the collapse in the gold price through Black Friday, 1869. The blackboard – from New York's Gold Room – was subsequently presented as evidence before a Congressional committee.

conspirators bought themselves a little extra credibility by hiring the US Ambassador to London, Robert C. Schenk, as a director. His name seemed a guarantee of good faith. Grant found out and warned his ambassador to sever his connection with the company: he did, but only after selling his own shares at a handsome profit.

The Crédit Mobilier Scandal had been several years in the making. The original fraud dated back to Abraham Lincoln's time. It was just Grant's luck that it began to surface during his term of office. Crédit Mobilier was a company set up to handle the construction of the western railroad on behalf of the Union Pacific Railroad itself. It had a captive client

and so could charge whatever price it liked. The sums it received were spent on Union Pacific shares, which were bought at face value before being sold on the stock market at many times their face amounts, reaping enormous gains for Crédit Mobilier's directors and their friends. Since the company recorded its profits in the par value of the shares it bought, its official returns, though perfectly respectable, were modest. Those who may have

Grant may have been innocent in the affair but it didn't say too much for his effectiveness in office. It was hardly the smartest move when, the following year, he awarded himself and his colleagues a major raise.

potentially have blown a whistle were quickly 'bought': shares were sold at par to Congressmen and officials who in their turn made small fortunes selling at market rates. No one wanted to kill the goose that laid the golden eggs. In the end, it was a squabble between directors that led to the inside story getting out to the press, just in time for Grant's 1872 election campaign. In all, it emerged, the company had charged $20 million ($362 million today) more than it had cost to build the Union

Pacific Railroad: the money had ended up in the pockets of corrupt financiers, officials and politicians.

Pay Rise

Grant may have been innocent in the affair but it didn't say too much for his effectiveness in office. It was hardly the smartest move when, the following year, he awarded himself and his colleagues in Congress a major raise. While his own salary shot up from $25,000 ($462,000 today) to $50,000 ($925,000), Senators' and Congressmen's went up from $5000 ($93,000 today) to $7500 ($139,000 today) – with a retroactive 'bonus' of another $5000 ($93,000 today). Since the President's salary may not by law be increased while he's in office, Grant's raise had to be hustled through in the four-day gap between his first

'The Dead, the Dying and the Crippled in the Crédit Mobilier Ward', as seen in the cartoon by Joseph Keppler. Respect for democratic institutions hit an all time low as the scale of wrongdoing emerged.

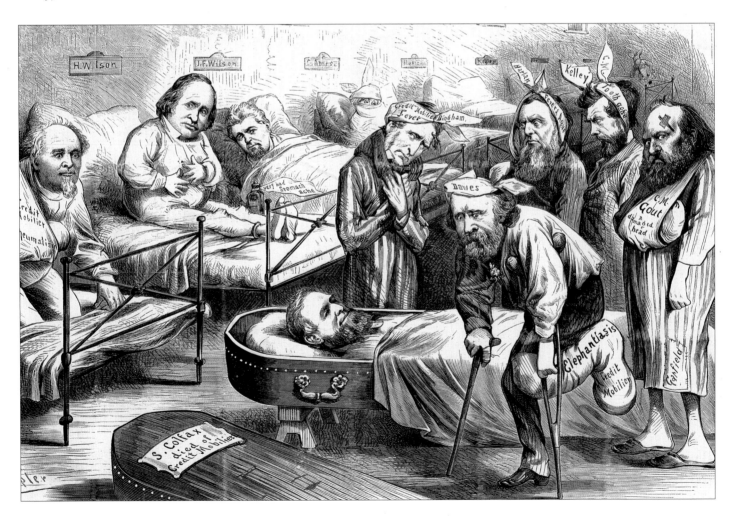

The Whiskey Ring trial finally got under way in October 1875 in the courthouse at Jefferson City, Missouri: the Federal Government had been defrauded of millions of dollars over several years.

and second term; Congress's 'bonus' seems to have been little more than a 'sweetener' to this deal. To add insult to injury, the bill was passed in secret and became public only through the vigilance of the press.

'Let No Guilty Man Escape'

The problem for the chronicler of Ulysses S. Grant's 'eight years of scandal' is that it gets hard to see where one outrage leaves off and another starts up. Corruption truly seems to have become endemic. Typically, the President himself comes out looking not quite guilty, but not quite innocent either – for how long could anyone, however blind and foolish, not have

known? Attorney Generals came and went – George H. Williams giving way to Edward Pierrepoint in 1875 – but the climate always seemed to be favourable for financial and official sleaze.

In 1875, the Whiskey Ring was discovered. Briefly, distillers in the Midwestern states had been dodging taxes for well over a decade. Whilst saving themselves (and robbing the US taxpayer of) many millions, they had been bribing Treasury officials to look the other way. The President seemed sincerely shocked: 'Let no guilty man escape,' he thundered ... till it emerged that the 'guilty men' included Orville E. Babcock, his private secretary and friend. Even now, with the integrity of government at stake, Grant's instinct was to close ranks, to protect his buddy. Babcock was brought to trial, but Grant doesn't seem to have understood the seriousness of what was happening. Prosecution witnesses were paid off; Grant took the stand in person to testify to Babcock's character. He was acquitted, but the Presidency had been dragged through the dirt.

Orville Babcock drew unwelcome attention from investigators again in 1876 over a case of graft involving business contracts. Phoney Secret Service agents working for the crooks broke into the home of the attorney spearheading the prosecution and planted incriminating evidence in the safe. A second set of burglars were then hired to break in and blow the safe. Having 'found' the planted evidence, they made their way to the house of another man, Columbus Alexander, a private citizen who'd been helping build the case against the conspirators. There they were arrested by the 'Secret Servicemen', gave up what they'd taken from the safe and said that Alexander had paid them to break into the Attorney's house, crack the safe and bring him what they found. An elaborate plan. Over-elaborate, perhaps, because one of the 'burglars' was quickly persuaded to turn state's witness by a suspicious prosecution, and the whole unseemly house of cards collapsed. Grant now got the message to the extent of 'distancing' himself quite literally from his sometime secretary, sending him to oversee the building of the Mosquito Inlet lighthouse in Florida. All the indications are, though, that his loyalty to his friend remained undimmed and that he'd have been brought back in from the cold (or, rather, the tropic heat) before too long. But Babcock's boat capsized in a storm while he was surveying the Mosquito Inlet site; he was drowned at the age of 48.

At one level, Grant appears to have sensed his disgrace: he'd failed in 'errors of judgement, not of intent', he pleaded in a letter to Congress. At another, he doesn't seem to have had a clue. Anxious to keep the gravy-train going, his political allies tried to get him to run for a third term. Congress quickly closed the door on that by passing legislation limiting Presidents to two terms. Even then, the hope remained that, after a few years

being fêted on the speaking-circuit in Europe (where he was still a war-hero), Grant would be able to return to power and it would be happy days again. Grant himself – a good old boy; not actively dishonest but passively, unconsciously corrupt – never appreciated how he'd let his country down after such sterling service.

An uncomfortable-looking trapeze-artist, President Grant holds up his henchmen. The Whiskey Ring Scandal left his administration without a leg to stand on: it was sustained only by his misplaced loyalty to his disgraced staff.

THE LOST PRESIDENTS: FRAUD AND FOLLY

We have to scratch about to find their achievements; we have to make an effort even to remember who they were. But the 'Lost Presidents' understood at least one aspect of their presidential role: they were well up to sleazy standard, that's for sure.

'I am a radical in thought (and principle) and a conservative in method (and conduct).'

After the tumults of the Civil War and the rancour of Reconstruction, America wanted nothing more than a quiet life. And, up to a point, it was to get it. So much so that the series of leaders who held office from the late-1870s to the early 1890s have often been referred to as the 'Lost Presidents'. They don't deserve to be forgotten, in fact, particularly in a history of Presidential scandal, for

Chester Arthur (left) was a product of a New York public administration system that saw government as interchangeable with grand larceny. He completed his education in corruption as Vice President to James A. Garfield (above).

some of what went on during their reigns was as squalid as anything before or since.

RUTHERFORD B. HAYES, 1877–81

It is perhaps appropriate enough that the shabby and shambolic Presidency of Ulysses S. Grant should have been followed by one of the most controversial and confusing elections in US history. Ironically, though, Hayes had established a reputation as a man of the utmost probity over many years: this had been his appeal to those who had cast their votes for him. And hundreds of thousands had done, seeing in Hayes the antidote America needed to the toxic corruption which had taken so strong a hold. Though acclaimed for his courage during his Civil War service, he'd remained every inch the simple soldier – quietly conscientious. Though a trained lawyer, with the beginnings of a career in Ohio state politics, he still seemed very much an outsider – in a good way.

His popularity wasn't surprising, then – but neither was it quite enough to get him to the White House unassisted. Indeed, by any obvious measure, his opponent won. A New Yorker, Democrat Samuel J. Tilden had won respect for the way he'd battled against corruption in his home city, so he too seemed a 'good guy' after Grant. He had come out on top in terms of total vote – with a margin of a quarter of a million votes. Of course, said insiders, it's never quite that simple. But Tilden had also secured a majority of electoral college votes – 184 as against Hayes' 165. Just one short of what he needed to win outright.

The Electoral Commission set up by Congress to come to a ruling on the Presidency shone an unwelcome light on American democracy in action. Especially because of the four states in which the result remained unresolved (Oregon, Florida, Louisiana and South Carolina), three were in the South. The Union Army still held sway down here – and Republican officials were still assiduously cooking the election results, disqualifying votes that didn't suit them and intimidating electors. Not that the Southern Democrats were any better: African-Americans brave enough to cast their votes had to run the gauntlet of violent mobs. Feelings were still running high, and Southern politicians of both stripes tended to feel justified in doing whatever it took to win: electoral fraud was rife, accordingly.

Not surprisingly, the Electoral Commission divided along party lines. Hayes' eight Republicans edged it over the seven Democrats. The Commission's conclusions were inconclusive, then, but Hayes won his opposition over by promising to bring Reconstruction to an end and withdraw the Union Army from the South. 'His Fraudulency' was duly declared President – and Tilden was cast aside. Some talked of a second Civil War, but wiser counsels prevailed and the Democrats decided to make the best of a bad job.

And not really quite so bad, after all, when they reflected that they'd secured the end they'd sought to Reconstruction and all that meant in terms of the restored autonomy of the South. They also had an

Rutherford Hayes was beyond reproach, a model of personal integrity by presidential standards. Despite his strenuous efforts, however, he couldn't stamp out the corruption that appeared to have become endemic in American public life.

invaluable stick with which to beat a President who, as straight as a die, could never feel comfortable in his position and never ceased to cringe to hear himself referred to as 'Old Eight to Seven'.

The Usurper in Office

As President, Hayes was every bit as trustworthy as he'd promised. No significant scandal marked his term. In deference to the feelings of First Lady 'Lemonade Lucy', the Hayes White House was dry (exceptions were made for the visits of one or two

> He felt strongly that the temptation of a second term made that impossible. How could a President hoping to secure re-election not be swayed by considerations of crowd-pleasing populist policies? How was such a man to take the tough decisions?

foreign leaders). Lucy Hayes was a devout Methodist, and held prayer-meetings every morning and invited her husband's colleagues to come and sing hymns with the First Family on Sunday nights.

In token of his intentions to do right by America, Rutherford Hayes had signed a statement before taking office vowing that under no circumstances would he allow himself to be persuaded to stand for re-election. 'He serves his party best who serves his country best,' he said at his inauguration. He felt strongly that the temptation of a second term made that impossible. How could a President hoping to secure re-election not be swayed by considerations of crowd-pleasing populist policies? How was such a man to take the tough decisions?

Railroaded Back to Work

Just a few months into his Presidency, the American economy – already suffering after four years in the recession – was threatened with more or less total shutdown when thousands of railroad workers went on strike. The Baltimore & Ohio Railroad had cut wages twice in quick succession; workers on other railroads

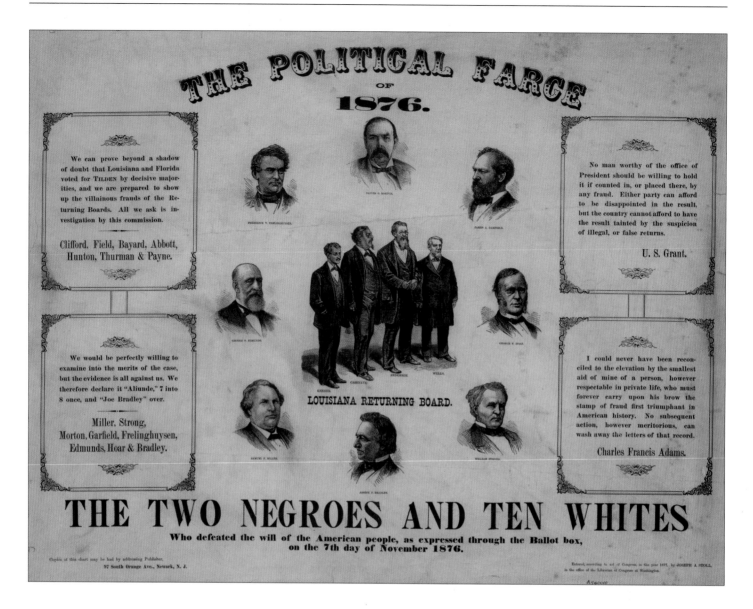

A Democratic Party poster names the guilty men who, it believed (with some justification), had 'stolen' the election of 1876 on Hayes' behalf. The incorruptible Hayes could never quite live down the manner of his election.

had downed tools in their support. America's workers generally felt they didn't have a voice. The controversial manner of Hayes' election only convinced them that the Republican elite would run America to suit itself: a great deal more was at stake for them than hourly pay. But then from Hayes' perspective a great deal more was at stake than the workings of the railroads. Since the strikers were blockading trains to prevent their use by blackleg labour, the movement of raw materials and finished goods was at a standstill, other industrial workers were coming out in sympathy, and the economy was grinding to a halt.

The President was resolute – ruthless, even. He gave the order that the authorities should break up crowds of strikers and force a way through for the trains to start moving once again. But local police forces, with their roots in the communities they served, didn't much fancy firing on their friends and neighbours: the President's tough talk was only making him look helpless. State militias were sent in, but in many cases they too shrank from violence. Only when Federal troops were dispatched to the centres of the strike was the Great Railroad Strike defeated, and order restored – amid scenes of shocking violence – after 45 days and 70-odd fatalities.

Mail Malfeasance

There was scarcely a whiff of any other scandal during Hayes' term in the White House: he'd selected his staff

SIOUX STAND-OFF

ITS OWN INTERNAL DIVISIONS so painfully settled, the United States had been free to pursue the war against America's native peoples. By now the theatre had shifted to the Great Plains, ancestral home to the Lakota Sioux. In a bitter war of 1866–7, Red Cloud's warriors had apparently won the right for their people to remain in their Dakota homelands, but then in 1874 General Custer's Expedition discovered gold in the Black Hills. Rather than stop the Gold Rush that resulted, the government insisted that the Lakota should make way, moving westward to new territories in the Upper Missouri Valley. Red Cloud tried hard to be flexible – as, in fairness, did Hayes himself – but neither man could carry his more

militant supporters with him. On the one hand Crazy Horse and Sitting Bull felt a principle was at stake, for which it was worth fighting to the death; on the other, many in the military felt the Sioux should simply be driven out by force. While Hayes looked hard for a compromise, the matter was increasingly taken out of his hands: soon both sides had set out along the road that would lead to Little Bighorn – and, ultimately, to Wounded Knee.

US Government officials had reached agreement with representatives of the Lakota at Fort Laramie in 1868, but the so-called Sioux Treaty had not proved adequate for a rapidly developing situation in the West.

Under the demanding domestic reign of the hard-praying, hard-hymn-singing, temperance-campaigning 'Lemonade Lucy' Hayes, the routines of everyday life in the White House were almost comically correct.

were essentially *ad hoc* arrangements. The scope for corruption was clearly immense, and unscrupulous postmasters had taken full advantage, it turned out. Hayes does appear to be at fault here to the extent that he was slow to see how deliberately and systematically the US taxpayer was being defrauded – he seems for a long time to have seen the problem as one of unfortunate but innocent inefficiency and waste.

Canal Corruption

Where more naked wrongdoing was in question, he was decisive in his response. He sacked his Secretary of the Navy, Richard W. Thompson, without the slightest hesitation. True, as far as Hayes was concerned, he'd been left with no real alternative. He'd specifically asked Thompson not to get involved with Ferdinand de Lesseps' scheme for a Panama Canal. The Frenchman was buoyed up by his recent success in Suez and saw a Panama Canal as a natural next step. Hayes didn't disagree, but wanted any such project to fly the Stars and Stripes. He forbade his staff from any involvement in the scheme. But Thompson couldn't resist the salary of $25,000 ($555,000 today) offered by the Frenchman for chairing a US 'advisory committee' – basically, a lobbying body designed to help allay American fears. Hayes saw it as a Trojan horse, and Thompson's agreement to participate as a clear act of defiance: he dismissed his naval chief without a moment's pause.

In the event, no one was to build the canal – at least not completely – for the moment. A more challenging project than anyone had anticipated, it took Teddy Roosevelt's drive to bring it to completion a quarter of a century later.

One day, it was to be a truly historic achievement. For decades, though, the Panama Canal represented rather too tough a challenge – not just to technology and finance but to public ethics.

well, and for the most part they knew better than to try anything untoward. Not that corruption could ever be entirely absent from the American scene: it emerged in 1879 that lavish postal subsidies were being stolen. In the Eastern and Midwestern states letters were by now, being carried in bulk by mail, under standardized procedures. Farther west, though, there were 'Star Routes' (so-called from the asterisks that marked them out as special and, essentially, provisional). On these, mail was carried in coaches, wagons or by men on horseback – in short, any way that it could, in what

JAMES GARFIELD, 1881

James Garfield served as President for just 199 days, but that was plenty of time for a man so at ease with sleaze to contribute to the history of White House scandal. He already had an impressive track record in this regard, having been among those Congressmen who'd been implicated in the Crédit Mobilier Scandal during the Grant administration. His close associate Thomas J. Brady (subsequently appointed to a senior position in the US Mail) had been implicated in the Star Routes Scandal of 1879. Garfield had also taken a $5000 ($111,000 today) retainer for legal advice from a company that hoped for the contract to provide wooden cobbles for paving DC's streets; as he pointed out, though, the contract hadn't in any sense been in his gift.

His election was controversial too – though it's only fair to say not only that it was pretty much a shoo-in after Hayes', and that he himself was as much sinned against as sinning. True, his supporters had opened up a slush fund for the express purpose of buying votes; they also blackmailed businessmen with threats of intrusive inspections and shook down public office-holders – if they wanted to keep their jobs, it was made clear that they'd better contribute. His running-mate Chester A. Arthur, the man who put the 'vice' in the Vice-Presidency, was disarmingly frank about the way the Republicans had bought the normally Democratic state of Indiana. At

James Garfield's presidency was, of course cut short in the cruellest possible way, but not before he'd established his credentials as one of the most corrupt and cynical of US Presidents.

Lucretia Rudolph-Garfield seems to have had a thankless and frustrating married life. Her husband made no real pretence of putting her first in his affections or in his plans, and they spent much of their time apart.

the same time, however, Garfield was definitely a victim of Democrat 'dirty tricks'. These included the forging of a letter purporting to show his support for the lifting of restrictions on Chinese immigration, to drive down labour costs in California and America at large.

Unlike Hayes, moreover, when the results were in, he could claim a majority of votes cast (albeit only 9000 on a nine-million poll). His electoral college vote was altogether more convincing (214 votes as against 155 for his Democratic Party rival). So his title to the Presidency was a great deal more secure than his predecessor's, even if, character-wise, he seemed distinctly dubious.

My Wife Doesn't Understand Me

Garfield's marriage was a compromise. First Lady Lucretia Rudolph-Garfield was intellectual – and a bit uptight. The future President had flagged his ambivalence toward her from early on in their engagement. When, in 1854, she arrived at Williams College, Massachusetts, to acclaim her fiancé's graduation, she was taken aback to find another woman with him, showing every indication of being romantically attached. Garfield confessed that he'd been having an affair with Rebecca Selleck – Lucretia was intimidating and cold toward him, he complained – but they patched things up and four years later the marriage went ahead, only for the groom to start putting distance between himself and his supposed soulmate almost immediately. With Garfield busy about his work as representative in the Ohio State legislature – and apparently in no great hurry to come home between-times – they spent only six weeks together in the first six years of their marriage. Lucretia was fed up being left alone to look after not only a difficult mother-in-law but Almeda Booth, a

Innocent bystanders in the train station waiting room stand frozen in shock as Charles J. Guiteau guns down the President at close-range. The assassin was the classic misfit: a loner, a drifter and an oddball.

doting former teacher of her husband's who was living with them as a lodger. But she was still more upset when she subsequently discovered that, some time early in 1863, while he was away on Army service in the Civil War, he'd had an affair with Lucia Calhoun, a young reporter with the *New York Times*.

Close Companions
Months later, Garfield went to Washington to take up a place in the House of Representatives. From that time on, the couple seem to have found their level with one another. They weathered the revelation of

the affair with Lucia Calhoun, which Garfield seems to have confessed in a fit of guilt: if anything, it appears to have enriched their relationship, as the cliché has it. Lucretia became an asset to her husband; his staunch supporter and his close companion. She made a hit as First Lady – at least in her first days. Within weeks, unfortunately, she'd been struck down by a severe bout of malaria, which incapacitated her for what little remained of her husband's term of office.

That was cruelly cut short, of course, on 2 July, when Charles Guiteau shot Garfield. He ambushed

him at the station, where Garfield had gone to catch a train to New Jersey, planning to have some time with Lucretia. Garfield fought for his life for the next three months (it has been suggested that incompetent doctoring did him more damage than Guiteau's bullets) but on 19 September 1881, he died.

An Odd Assassin

Charles J. Guiteau had (to use today's terminology) 'stalked' President Garfield for some time. He'd even crashed a White House Reception and spoken to the First Lady. He'd pursued a peculiar path through the American society of the time, since failing to get into the University of Michigan in 1857. His father, in fairness, appears to have been odder even than Charles himself: he now bombarded his son with literature for the Oneida Community in upstate New York. This strange 'church' had been founded by John Humphrey Noyes in 1848. Christ's heavenly dominion not only

> With Garfield busy about his work as representative in the Ohio State legislature – and apparently in no great hurry to come home between times – they spent only six weeks together in the first six years of their marriage.

could but should be realized, Noyes told his flock: his community was a paradise on earth. But had not Christ Himself said that there would be no marriage after the Resurrection (Matthew 22, 30)? For this reason, they would practice 'free love' at Oneida. Boys were to be initiated by older women as they came of age; he himself took responsibility for the sexual education of the virgin girls and exercised control thereafter by ruling on who should sleep with whom.

No one, unfortunately, seemed to want to sleep with Charles J. Guiteau, who enrolled in the community some time in the early 1860s; neither did he want to perform the manual labour expected of male adherents. In 1865, he left, attempting to sue the community for alleged loss of earnings – though in

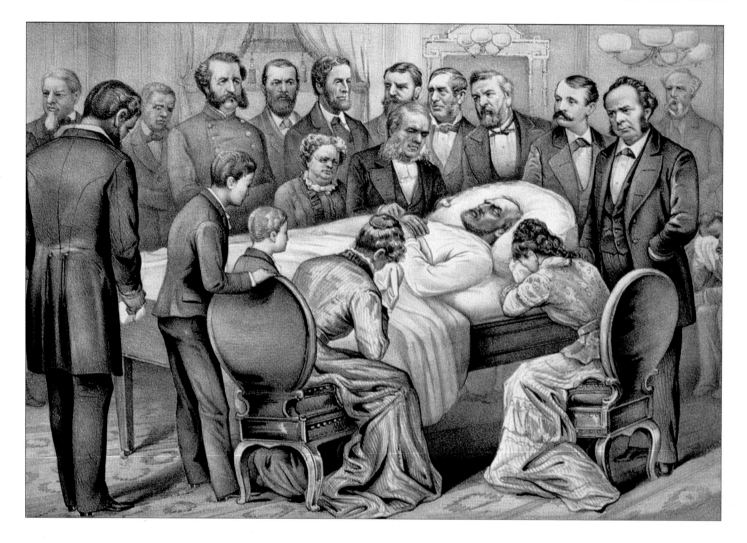

what profession it was as yet by no means clear. At first, Guiteau set up as a lawyer in Chicago. Unfortunately he was about as successful in this role as he was in his next one, as revivalist preacher. By 1874, he'd been married – and divorced, having caught syphilis in an encounter with a prostitute. By the decade's end he'd washed up in Washington. Having badgered a succession of officials, he seems first to have persuaded himself that he'd been promised a

Trailing the President to the railroad station one day, and in a position to shoot him, Guiteau stayed his hand because Mrs Garfield was ill, so it didn't seem considerate to kill her husband.

Despite the violent abruptness of Guiteau's attack, Garfield was to have a slow lingering death. He was finally done for not by the assassin's bullet but by his doctors' treatment, some suggested.

government job, then formed a fixed conviction that Garfield's administration had let him down. Before long, he'd come to the conclusion that God wanted Garfield killed.

Even then he was an odd assassin. Trailing the President to the railroad station one day, and in a position to shoot him, Guiteau stayed his hand because Mrs Garfield was ill, so it didn't seem the most considerate time to kill her husband. By the time his trial came round, he had so far departed from all sense of reality that he was looking forward to his release: his first plan was to run for President himself. In the event, the nearest thing to a campaigning platform he was destined to mount was the executioner's scaffold: he was hanged on 30 June 1882.

CHESTER ARTHUR, 1881–5

If Garfield seems to have experienced a moral turnaround in his attitude toward his wife, this was nothing next to Chester Arthur's transformation. As cynical a campaigner as they come, he'd started out in politics as protégé of Roscoe Conkling, the New York power broker, and been promoted to the job of Collector of the Port of New York by Ulysses S. Grant. Conkling remained a background presence in Arthur's career – so much so that there were even suggestions that he'd actually organized Garfield's assassination so his 'client' could rule, while he held power behind the throne. An ingenious theory, but as we've seen, Charles J. Guiteau had needed no encouragement or direction from anybody else; nor is there any reason to think that Conkling – or Arthur – however corrupt, were of murderous intent.

In truth, the most important thing which Arthur appears to have gained from his mentor was a comprehensive understanding of government corruption and how it worked. He'd learned his trade in the Customs House, of course: officials routinely dipped their fingers in the till. No problem, as long as they passed a portion of their profits on to him. Not that he was interested (or *only* interested) in personal gain; the party was important too, since politics was about power – and all the profit that could bring. Public officials, he knew, were there to serve the politicians, not the people; and as the price of their

The 'Dude President' takes a luxurious ride. Elegance like Arthur's didn't come cheap, of course, but by this time bribes and backhands had become accepted as an inseparable part of public life.

offices, they were to be milked for party funds.

Old habits die hard, and longstanding friendships are difficult to renounce: corrupt practices continued into the Arthur Presidency. But the 'spoilsmen' had a surprise in store: when, in 1882, they introduced an $18 million (390 million today) scheme supposedly to 'improve waterways' in key Congressional districts, Arthur vetoed what was quite clearly a 'pork barrel' measure aimed to create new jobs and offices where votes and influence were needed. Congress took no notice of the veto, and, voting again, passed the legislation notwithstanding. But the President had served notice of change to come.

It still came as an enormous shock when the poacher turned gamekeeper once and for all, Arthur

A 'Presidential Conjuror' in the view of *Puck* magazine, Arthur astonished all observers by the adroitness with which he found inducements for all the different political constituencies on whose support he would rely for his election.

throwing his full Presidential weight behind the Pendleton Act. This legislation was passed in 1883 as a direct attack on government corruption. It was limited in scope, applying only to Federal positions, not to the more plentiful, more freely abused state offices, but it spelled the beginning of the end for the time-dishonoured 'spoils system'. Rather than being in the gift of incoming administrations, these offices were to be the property of a permanent civil service, through which people would rise not by political allegiance but by merit. A system of exams would help ensure that key positions went to the best-qualified candidates.

Corruption will always find a way, of course, and American political parties their funding. Unable to offer individuals incentives to contribute, they turned to businesses instead, making all sorts of dodgy deals. But the Pendleton Act can at the very least be seen as an important declaration of intent; an acknowledgement that government should not be for sale.

TO THE VICTOR, THE SPOILS

UNTIL THE PENDLETON ACT, the American civil service had been run according to the 'spoils system': the winning party named its own people for important roles. To our eyes, it wasn't just corrupt but overtly so. The idea that it ought to be changed seemed genuinely challenging to many: why would a man of wealth and importance give his money and lend his influence to a campaign if not in hopes of some reward? For public offices were frankly viewed as moneymaking opportunities. If there weren't legitimate fees to be collected, there were under-the-counter bribes.

Hence too, in turn, the logic behind the political levy system. If a man was coining it in thanks to a position he'd got from the Republicans or Democrats, why shouldn't he be expected to contribute to that party's funds? And so it went on in a self-perpetuating cycle, the officials feeling entitled to their embezzlements, the politicians feeling entitled to their cut.

GROVER CLEVELAND, 1885–9 & 1893–7

So, were the good times over for graft? For a while, it almost seemed they might be. Grover Cleveland found other ways of offending against morality. By training a lawyer and a bachelor-about-Buffalo in the 1870s, he made the best of his single status, spending much of his time in bars and saloons. An affair with an attractive young widow, Maria Halpin, produced a child – he was never convinced he was the father, though she called him Oscar Cleveland. He acknowledged his responsibility – if not his paternity – and when her deepening alcoholism prevented her carrying out a mother's duties, he arranged for her to be hospitalized, and paid for the boy to be placed in an orphanage.

Despite a stint as Sheriff of Erie County between 1871 and 1874, Cleveland reached the age of 40 with no real political ambitions. In 1881, however, at the age of 44, he allowed himself to be talked into running for office in Buffalo as a reforming mayor on the Democrats' behalf. His subsequent rise was meteoric – so impressed were voters by his effectiveness in fighting graft at local level that calls soon followed for him to perform on a wider stage. It was next stop Albany as, in 1882, he got himself elected Governor; again he was a new broom, sweeping corruption clean. In 1884, he secured the Presidential nomination – his Republican opponent was James G. Blaine.

As with Hayes before him, Cleveland could make his inexperience a virtue: he was an outsider, untouched and untarnished by Washington and its ways. Blaine had been around the block a few too many times: there were rumours that he'd been too cosily (and profitably) involved with major railroad companies. The Republicans weren't shy about bringing up the case of Cleveland's 'orphan' son, and it was indeed too delicious a scandal not to catch the public interest. Cleveland was honest enough to admit his faults – and smart enough to see the

> Cleveland was honest enough to admit his faults – and smart enough to see the futility of concealment. His frank admission seems to have won him great respect.

futility of concealment. His frank admission seems to have won him great respect. When it came to the crunch, the people were prepared to overlook a private (and conscientiously atoned-for) personal transgression to elect a man they trusted to see to the public good.

Grover the Good?

'Ma, Ma, where's my pa? Gone to the White House, ha, ha, ha!' The delighted chant in Pennsylvania Avenue when Cleveland came to take up residence said it all. Whatever his past failings, there he was.

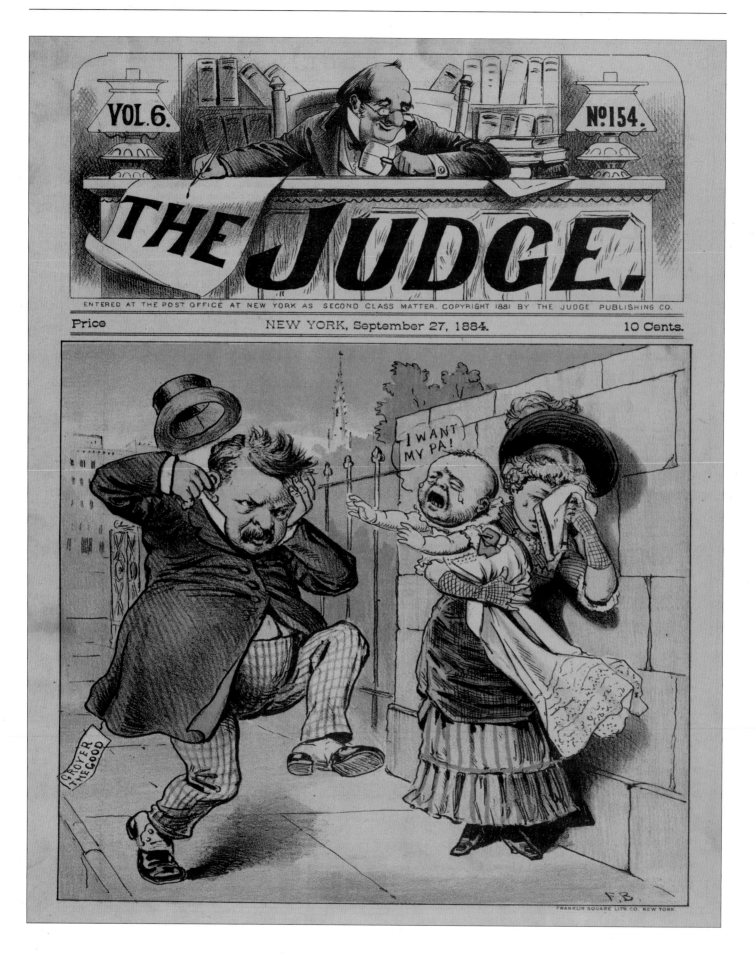

Left: 'I want my pa!', screams the baby boy – but it turned out that the electors wanted Cleveland too, whatever his flaws and his past transgressions were. They voted overwhelmingly for him in 1892.

Above: Soldiers put on a show of strength during the Pullman strike of 1894. Cleveland made victory for the employers a point of principle – hard as it is to see how national security was at stake.

His present failings were perhaps a lack of wider imagination and compassion. His desire to do away with the Pork Barrel and get voters value for money could go too far. He saw it as a stand of principle when in 1887 he vetoed a bill providing for $10,000 ($216,000 today) to be spent on fresh seed corn for farmers in drought-ridden Texas. But real, suffering (and taxpaying) families were in the direst need. And in another echo of Hayes' reign, he sent federal troops to Chicago to break the Pullman Strike of 1894: 'If it takes the entire army and navy of the United States to deliver a postcard in Chicago, that card will be delivered.' It didn't take quite that much, but 12,000 troops were deployed alongside Federal Marshals and Illinois State Guardsmen. In the violence that followed, 13 were killed and 57 injured. The labour-relations issue aside, there was also a racial angle – so

many of the Pullman attendants were African-Americans that this felt like (and arguably amounted to) an attack by white authority on black employees seeking justice. But Cleveland's response raised more fundamental constitutional questions – most bluntly: by what right did a President intervene in such a dispute?

Furthermore, Cleveland's response to 'Coxey's Army' showed an almost vindictive attitude to organized labour. This group of unemployed workers had marched to Washington to call for assistance for the hungry, and for job-creating investment in highway construction and other public works. Cleveland believed it was up to government and business to sort out America's problems. It was up to workers to work, not to ask questions or make demands. Cleveland had the marchers harassed by Federal Marshals as they made their trek from the West; when they arrived in Washington, the National Guard turned out and arrested the ringleaders for walking on the grass beside the Capitol.

Cleveland couldn't prevail against the economic crisis that he had inherited or the popular animosity his hard-line dealings had provoked. Yet, though he was ousted in 1889, he was back in office four years later. The American electorate had apparently forgiven, if not forgotten. He may well have wished he'd quit while he was ahead. Economic conditions were hardly any better than they'd been, while he himself was suffering ill-health. Increasingly, he slumped into a state of depression. And if he felt beleaguered, he really was.

THE RECORD BREAKER

FRANCES FOLSOM CLEVELAND was the first First Lady to have married her President in the White House. Her husband snatched a moment from his hectic schedule to plight his troth. Just 21 when she wed, she became the youngest ever First Lady, a title she retains to this day. She was her spouse's junior by 27 years, but this isn't quite a record: John Tyler had been 30 years older than Julia Gardiner, his second wife.

Below: Grover Cleveland and his Cabinet had to govern in tough times, when there were tough decisions to make. Many Americans felt that they lacked compassion in the way they addressed the economic crisis.

Right: Cleveland's First Lady, Frances Folsom, was fully 21 years his junior. No doormat, though, she even rewrote the traditional marriage vows, pledging to 'love and honour' – but not to 'obey' – her husband.

Americans were hurting, and feeling angry. Attacks on the White House were increasing – just odd bricks and bottles, really, but the potential threat was there. Security was stepped up. Once the President's residence had been a semi-public place, but now it was surrounded with high railings and the wrought iron gates were locked.

BENJAMIN HARRISON, 1889–93

It's been Benjamin Harrison's unfortunate destiny to be a Lost President even among Lost Presidents – his reward for managing to topple Cleveland first time round (albeit only by an electoral college vote). His single term has to a considerable extent slipped from sight, straddled and squeezed by Grover Cleveland's two; he seems the more inconspicuous for having in any case clearly been selected as the Republicans'

Cleveland-lookalike candidate. James G. Blaine had still been the big-hitter in the Republican Party through Cleveland's first term; only gradually had his backers become resigned to the fact that their champion was too tarnished.

As Cleveland had done before him, Harrison came from nowhere (politically speaking; geographically, he remains the only President to have come from Indiana). He had no baggage of corruption to carry; and he promised to crack down on graft. Like Cleveland, he sprang from a Presbyterian background – Cleveland's father, in fact, had been a preacher in that church. But where Cleveland had early on to a

John Wanamaker did his friend Benjamin Harrison no favours at all by giving him a holiday cottage: the generous gift gave rise to the chief scandal of an otherwise largely blameless administration.

large extent left his religious background by the wayside, Harrison remained devout – it mattered as much to him to be a Presbyterian Elder as a President.

He made a point of his reforming zeal: the centrepiece of his policies was the reinforcement of the Pendleton Act and the extension of its coverage. But he couldn't always control the actions of his supporters. William Wade Dudley, the Treasurer of the Republican Party's National Committee, caused his campaign embarrassment during the elections when letters were leaked revealing plans to buy up votes in Indiana. At the end of Harrison's term as well, his supporters were to cause discomfort: in 1890, his Postmaster-General, John Wanamaker, with some friends from the Philadelphia business world, presented First Lady Caroline Harrison with a pretty little cottage on Cape May, on the Jersey coast. It was never clear what strings were attached, but when the gift was made public it certainly raised eyebrows. Harrison hastily insisted that he'd been planning to buy the cottage all along and that Wanamaker had merely been helping him out; he sent his friend a cheque for $10,000 ($243,000 today).

Looking After the Boys

Harrison's choice as overseer of veterans' pensions seemed inspired. James R. Tanner was himself war-disabled; an ex-Corporal, he'd lost both legs at the Battle of Bull Run. A man who understood the

Benjamin Harrison was probably as pure a spirit as ever held high office in the United States – despite this, he found himself accused of corruption, thanks to the overzealous efforts of his supporters.

> A man who understood the problems veterans faced, then, and who could be trusted to have the veterans' interests at heart. Boy, did he have the veteran's interests at heart!

problems veterans faced, then, and who could be trusted to have the veterans' interests at heart. Boy, did he have their interests at heart! While not himself corrupt, fatally he seems to have failed to grasp the role of government and the resources at its command. Making a boast of his promise to 'treat the boys liberally', he saw it as his duty to shower any vets he could track down with largesse – including many who hadn't even applied for assistance. In a matter of months, his department had gone massively over-budget. Harrison was forced to sack him within a year.

VI

WORLD POWER: IN BED WITH INDUSTRY

The closing years of the nineteenth century saw the United States come of age not only as an economic giant but as a major modern nation with imperial ambitions, but if America's power was growing, so was its potential to do harm.

◆

'In the time of darkest defeat, victory may be nearest.'

The Pendleton Act, as we've already seen, gave a different emphasis to American political life. The effect, at first subtle, was cumulatively overwhelming. Jobs which had once been bought and sold as the personal property of rich individuals were now the preserve of a meritocratically-ordered bureaucracy. But, at least until Heaven felt like sending down a new species of public representative – honest, altruistic and dedicated to public service for its own sake – the money to grease the political

Leon Czolgosz (left) is held behind bars before his execution for the assassination of William McKinley (above). His crime got the history of the Presidency in the twentieth-century off to a distinctly ropey start.

machinery had to come from somewhere. So it's at about this time that we see the start of an intimate (at times even incestuous) relationship between politics and business: what left-wing critics call 'Corporate America' was born.

WILLIAM MCKINLEY, 1897–1901

Too nice a guy to be President, perhaps, McKinley could never really get over the obligation he had to 'Dollar Mark' Hanna, the man who'd been his 'kingmaker'. Hanna had organized McKinley's campaign, scaring business witless with horror stories about Democrat William J. Bryan's intentions to tie the US Dollar to the 'silver standard'. In fairness, what amounted to a relaxation in economic rigour was bound to be inflationary. Whilst this would suit the South and its farmers – net debtors, they'd find it easier to keep up with their payments – it would

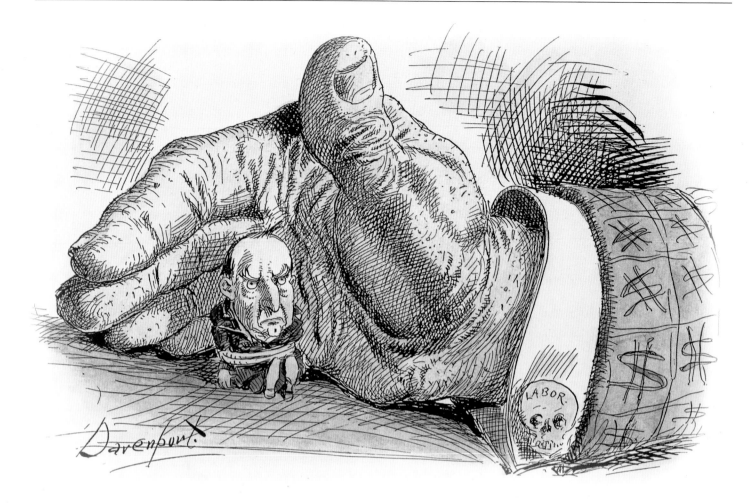

reduce the export value of what North-eastern industry produced. On the other hand, McKinley's eagerness to increase tariffs on imports was anti-competitive; the 'protection' it offered US industry was in the long term arguably illusory, and it hit agriculture hard by raising the cost of machinery.

Lobbying hard with business donors, Hanna raised huge funds with which he produced a voluminous campaign literature of leaflets promoting the gold standard and prophesying doom of every description if it should be dropped. In truth, there's nothing so very different in what he did to what campaigns do invariably (and more or less legitimately) now – he was playing hardball, sure, but he wasn't guilty of misconduct. The problem for McKinley was more that his mentor's profile was so high that he himself was seen as a puppet. People couldn't take him seriously enough as President.

And that impression was only reinforced once McKinley was in office, when pressure was put on the veteran Senator for Ohio, John Sherman, to vacate his seat. The Governor of Ohio then put Hanna's name

The satirical point could hardly be clearer: McKinley is shown quite literally in the palm of 'Dollar Mark' Hanna's hand. He was never able to live down his association with the notorious power broker.

forward for the Senate and he was able to take his place as Senator for that state. Sherman was more than compensated for his sacrifice by his appointment to the position of Secretary of State. Unfortunately, he wasn't remotely equal to the task. Aged 74, he was physically doddery and his memory was failing: he'd forget where he was up to and lose track of the discussion in top-level talks. Within a year, he'd had to be replaced by William R. Day.

'A Splendid Little War'

But if McKinley's Presidency seems scandalous now, it's not so much for corruption in the traditional sense as for the foreign-policy decisions his administration made. It was on his watch that, in 1898, the notorious sinking of the USS *Maine* took place. The battleship blew up and sank in Havana harbour, with 260 hands.

All the indications are that, as the Spanish authorities insisted at the time, an accidental explosion on board had sent the *Maine* to the bottom, but the Americans decided to suspect skulduggery on Spain's part. Cuba had long been coveted and this seemed the perfect opportunity to invade and take possession from a Spain which had been on the decline for decades now. A frankly one-sided Spanish–American War was brought to an end after 113 days. William R. Day argued scrupulously that, with the exception of Cuba, the Spanish colonies should be returned: he was relieved of his position for his pains. Instead, America helped itself to Puerto Rico, Guam and the Philippines. A nice little return on what had been, in

The sinking of the USS *Maine* was a tragic accident that killed nearly three-quarters of her crew, it appears – though there was no way America was going to admit as much with a quarrel to be picked and Cuba to be won.

But if McKinley's Presidency seems scandalous now, it's not so much for corruption in the traditional sense as for the foreign-policy decisions his administration made.

the words of Day's replacement as Secretary of State, John Hay, 'a splendid little war'.

It had its less splendid aspects, though. With the US press whipped up to a fury beforehand about stories of Spanish atrocities in Cuba, McKinley had been criticized for not taking a tough enough line from the start. At the same time, he'd been taken to task for a buccaneering foreign policy. What's an empire-building

Mark Hanna watches as McKinley struggles, having bitten off more Cuban cigar than he can comfortably smoke. Though bloodied and bandaged, the President managed to pass the blame on to his Secretary of War.

President to do? Claims of Spanish outrages, though much exaggerated, had been by no means completely untrue. What we would now call an 'asymmetric war', it pitched a conventionally powerful Spanish occupying army against a guerrilla force deeply embedded in the island's population, amongst which it was hard to make out who was friend (or at least 'civilian') and who was foe.

This was precisely the problem faced by the American force sent to take possession of the Philippines, after the decision had been made to keep that colony. Not surprisingly, they won the conventional battle, securing the islands with the loss of just over 4000 lives as against five times that number on the Filipino side. Actually enforcing their rule over the Philippines was infinitely harder, though, and there's no doubt that US forces ended up resorting to terror tactics, deploying machine guns against village warriors armed with bows and spears; capturing, torturing and shooting 'suspects' ('Kill anyone over ten,' came the order from General Jacob Smith): ultimately up to a million civilians were slaughtered. America should have been freeing the Filipinos, wrote the outraged novelist Mark Twain: instead it was enslaving them.
'I am opposed to having the eagle put its talons on any other land.'

SEIZURES AND SLIPPERS

IDA SAXTON MCKINLEY HAD BEEN a beauty when William met her in 1867, but she hadn't by any means been just a pretty face. Every inch the young lady, she'd gone to finishing school before going off on a European tour like a Henry James heroine, but she'd then started work as a cashier in her father's bank. At the time, this was regarded as very much a man's employment.

But Ida wasn't as tough as she seemed. In the 1870s she'd been knocked sideways by the deaths first of her mother and then of her two daughters – the first aged three, the second only six months. She'd become epileptic, prone to seizures at the most inopportune moments: one took her at her husband's inauguration ball. Increasingly retiring, she dedicated her life to crochet: she made slippers – thousands of pairs, which she gave as gifts.

Shifting the Blame

Victory in Cuba left America in a buoyant mood. But soon less happy stories started to trickle in. US troops on campaign in the mountains and forests had been woefully ill-prepared and ill-equipped. Though militarily it had been a pushover, with only 400 fatalities on the American side, many thousands had fallen sick and some 5000 even died. McKinley adroitly deflected all this criticism on to his Secretary of War, Russell A. Alger, who became the scapegoat for everything that had gone wrong.

Meanwhile, Mark Hanna's friends and protégés were moving in on lucrative opportunities in an island which America found more convenient to keep at arm's length as a nominally 'independent' client state. One, Estes C. Rathbone, had to be removed from his position as Director General of Posts when it turned out that $100,000 ($2.7 million today) had gone missing.

Mild-mannered to the last, McKinley died a magnanimous death, gunned down by the anarchist Leon Czolgosz in the course of a public appearance at the Pan-American Exposition in Buffalo, New York, on 6 September 1901. On feeling the bullets thud home, the President's first thought was for his First Lady: he asked his attendants to break the news to her gently. His second was for the welfare of his assassin. Czolgosz had been disarmed by an angry crowd, who by now were beating him so badly there were real fears that he might be killed. McKinley's compassion was misplaced – not so much because his murderer didn't deserve it as because Czolgosz was rescued only to be

McKinley's assassination stunned America. Czolgosz's attack could hardly have been more public. He shot the President on his way to an international exposition, in the presence of a considerable crowd.

tried, convicted and sent to the electric chair a few weeks later. The President was dead by then: he'd hung on for several days, giving his doctors hope he might be saved, but his wounds developed gangrene and he died on 14 September.

THEODORE ROOSEVELT, 1901–9

The title of President of the United States has conferred a historical aura on almost all its holders: in Teddy Roosevelt's case, though, perhaps uniquely, the man appears to have been bigger than the office. Certainly as far as colour was concerned. The expression 'larger than life' might have been minted for this ebullient, astonishingly energetic figure who found time not only to lend his name to a popular children's toy but also to start America's National Parks. Yet the conservationist was also a big-game hunter, the political theorist a man of action, the 'rough-rider' a writer of elegance and style. He personified to perfection that extravagant American complexity which had so famously been hymned by poet Walt Whitman in his 'Song of Myself' (1855).

American politics' cowboy hero, he'd actually served as a sheriff's deputy in North Dakota in the 1880s, You really couldn't have made him up. In October 1912, as an elder statesman, he took a would-be-assassin's bullet in the chest. Recognizing that the wound wouldn't be fatal and could wait, he had the outdoorsman's cool courage

It was almost inevitable that he would end up overspending for the Panama Canal.

(not to mention the born politician's sense of theatre) to stand speaking for an hour-and-a-half to a captivated crowd while the bloodstain slowly spread across his shirtfront.

A Question of Trust

But Roosevelt wasn't always strutting his stuff: he was an indefatigable legislator. As a New York State Assemblyman in the early 1880s, he drafted more bills than any other representative. He was also a committed fighter against corruption, taking on the vested interests of New York City's Police Department – then a rats' nest of nepotism, procedural abuse and graft. He also carved out a reputation as a trust-buster, attacking those big businesses who came together in cartels, or 'trusts', to fix their prices with each other, making a mockery of the ideas of capitalist competition or consumer choice. But then, characteristically, he contradicted himself – not, to be sure, because he was conventionally corrupt or avaricious, but because it seems so expansive a character couldn't see that the normal rules might apply to him. He was no bean-counter and it was almost

Writer, thinker, legislator, man of action ... Teddy Roosevelt was all these things and a great many more besides: not since Jefferson had quite such a compelling character occupied the presidency.

Right: Roosevelt in the Badlands. Sure, he was a poser, but he was also unmistakeably the real thing – whatever he claimed that to be. It's no surprise that his appeal to the electorate was irresistible.

inevitable that he would end up overspending for the Panama Canal. Epic projects demand epic gestures – and what gesture could be more epic than paying $40 million for an enterprise worth a tenth of that amount?

A courageous President Teddy Roosevelt refuses to be cowed by Colombia, who is seen here sporting a sombrero, in this ironic cartoon comment on America's imperial policies in Latin America and the Caribbean.

Suggestions were made that the President had been cut in on what he'd been well aware was a colossal overspend, but this was never proven – nor does it seem remotely typical of the man.

He wasn't a man to sweat the details, though, and a cynic might even say that he was capable of allowing himself to take advantage of this aspect of his own nature: everything's 'deniable' when your mind is fixed on the big picture. It's hard to doubt

that, at some level at least, he knew what he was doing when, in 1904, in his fight for re-election, he took his Secretary of Labor and Commerce George B. Cortelyou as his campaign manager. Cortelyou, an old hand, knew where big business's bodies were buried and could extract contributions pretty much by force. This funding did a great deal to help Roosevelt to his landslide triumph. And then, in 1907, in backing the merger between US Steel and

> Roosevelt's assumption that the rules were there to be broken (at least by him) surely had some justification at this particular moment, with panic reigning on the stock-market. However inconsistent, his actions helped head off a major slump.

A project of inordinate ambition and expense, the Panama Canal was bound to appeal to Teddy Roosevelt: shown here with workmen on the ground, he made its completion a consuming goal.

Tennessee Coal and Iron, the rough-rider rode roughshod over the anti-trust laws he'd fought so tirelessly to protect. That said, Roosevelt's assumption that the rules were there to be broken (at least by him) surely had some justification at this particular moment, with panic reigning on the stock-market. However inconsistent, his actions helped head off a major slump.

Growing Grass
It was during Theodore Roosevelt's second term that Chitto Harjo came to Washington to speak to the Senate. His name meant 'Crazy Snake', and he was the Chief of the Muscogee Creek. His people, already forced to migrate from their ancestral homes in Alabama to Oklahoma's Indian Territory, were coming under pressure to move again to give way to settlers. Famously – or notoriously, perhaps – Chitto Harjo

recalled the words of a tribal elder who'd told him he could trust the word of the white man, because of the treaties he had made.

It didn't last quite that long, of course. The Creek were moved on a few years later. The 'Crazy Snake Uprising' of 1909 was quickly suppressed – without bloodshed, thankfully. Roosevelt liked to think that he took a no-nonsense man-of-the-world's view of America's indigenous peoples – they were individuals like any others, some good, some bad, he said. It sounds fair-minded, but it was politically convenient as well. He was brusquely impatient of any suggestion that the Indians might have collective rights *as nations* and scoffed at what he called 'false sentimentality' about their plight.

Two top-hatted woodsmen, Ballinger and Blanchot go to war over the nation's trees: there were important issues of conservation (not to mention corruption) at stake, but most Americans did not understand them.

WILLIAM HOWARD TAFT, 1909–13

Weighing in at around 136kg (300lbs), William Howard Taft was America's heaviest President to date. 'Old Jumbo' was no lightweight politically either, come to that. True, he was slow on his feet, and easily outmanoeuvred by a 'millionaires' club' Senate which saw it as its duty to drag its feet over his anti-trust measures and his bid to bring anti-competitive import tariffs down. But his Presidency offers slim pickings to searchers after scandal: the most he can credibly be convicted of is misjudgement.

He certainly showed naivety over the Alaskan Land Speculation Scandal: this affair eventually split the Republican Party down the middle. On one side was Gifford Pichot, a distinguished conservationist whom

That rarity, a decent, honourable president, utterly straightforward in all his dealings, William Howard Taft still presided over political malfeasance: he could on occasion be too unworldly for his own good.

THERE'S ONLY A LITTLE DIFFERENCE BETWEEN THEM
From the *Meddler* (Cincinnati)

Theodore Roosevelt had placed in charge of the US Forest Service. On the other was Secretary of the Interior Richard Ballinger, suspected by Pichot of being in the pocket of big business. The two had come into conflict as early as 1905 over the suggestion that Ballinger had involved himself with an Idaho speculator setting out to purchase land in Alaska for mining coal. An agent of the General Land Office, who had been pursuing an investigation into the deal, had abruptly been dismissed from his position – apparently on Ballinger's intervention.

Taft took his Secretary of the Interior's part. What else could he do, he must have thought. It still blew up in his face in 1910. The agent went to the press and the whole tale came out; Gifford Pichot publicly backed the whistleblower, leaving Taft no alternative but to dismiss him and to appear to America as a protector of the corrupt.

WOODROW WILSON, 1913–21

Woodrow Wilson, another Presbyterian President, had an air of rectitude and steadiness that was only enhanced by his stint as President of Princeton University. So eager was he in his attacks on protectionist tariffs, trusts and other business abuses, that critics accused him of being a 'Bolshevik' – a reference to the revolutionaries on the brink of seizing power in Russia. The reality was that both great parties recognized the need to save capitalism from itself: true competition was needed, and real transparency for investors.

He was prepared to put honour before political advantage, for himself or for the United States. He stunned Congress in 1914 by telling them that he was going voluntarily to waive the right (claimed controversially and deeply dubiously by Taft) for American ships to use the Panama Canal for free. The previous year, he had refused to recognize the military government led to

power in Mexico by Victoriano Huerta after the murder of Francisco Madero, little as the Liberal leader had been to his administration's taste.

It might, of course, be objected that it was no business of a US President to take a position over who should or shouldn't have power in another sovereign state. But Woodrow Wilson was by temperament an interventionist, incapable of standing idly by. He intervened in Haiti, the Dominican

Stiff and formal in his self-presentation, Woodrow Wilson revealed an unexpected swashbuckling streak once he arrived in the White House, intervening in worldwide crises – not least, of course, World War I.

She was every inch the establishment hostess, but Edith Wilson's striking looks reminded those who met her of a more romantic ancestry – as a direct descendant of the Powhatan Princess Pocahontas.

> He was prepared to put honour before political advantage, for himself or for the United States.

Republic and in Mexico itself before sending soldiers to France to join the fighting in World War I. You wouldn't have thought it to look at him, but this quiet and academic-looking man was as swashbuckling in his way as Teddy Roosevelt had been – and as ready to break the rules if it came to that. His recruitment of corporate executives to aid in mobilizing America for the war in Europe gave rise to clear conflicts of interest: it was worth it, he insisted; the cause was just. Just as there had been at the outbreak of the Civil War, big (and hasty) contracts meant big profits for unscrupulous middlemen. Again, for Wilson, the end justified the means.

Woodrow's Women

Ellen Axson Wilson suffered from Bright's disease. Not surprisingly in the circumstances, she was depressed. This put a strain on her marriage with Woodrow

JIM CROW

IT'S EASY TO FORGET, given his later association with New Jersey, that Woodrow Wilson had spent much of his childhood in Georgia. It's easy to forget, given his general moral strenuousness and sense of honour, that he gave at the very least passive support to the march of segregation in the South.

Wilson could point to abolitionists among his ancestors, but the tone had been set by those in his family who'd served the Confederacy: his earliest boyhood memory was of an encounter with the dashing Southern general Robert E. Lee. It was

during his term of office that the 'Whites Only' signs went up outside restrooms and beside drinking fountains in Washington DC, and interracial marriages were outlawed. Further south, segregation had existed in practice for decades, but Federal buildings (post offices, law courts, etc) had at least offered some respite. Now, with the President's blessing, these last havens of decency had been whipped away. There were no institutions to which African-Americans could now look in the hope of a better life.

Wilson for a great many years before she died in the White House in 1914. The very next year, he married Edith Galt Wilson, who could claim the distinction of being a direct descendant of the famous Native American Princess Pocahontas.

So quickly did Wilson wed his second First Lady, however, that the Washington gossips hinted at an earlier involvement: had Wilson really been off with his late love before being on with the new? Had he even had her murdered? All sorts of rumours circulated in a Washington in which gossip was fast and febrile at the best of times and which could hardly contain its scandalized excitement at the

> Intense as they are, though, they leave unclear the question of whether what was clearly an 'emotional affair' was ever consummated. The evidence is circumstantial, nothing more.

strait-laced President's remarriage. All the indications are, however, that it was more a matter of the President's being lost without a woman to look to for company and reassurance. Their letters suggest that the apparently uptight President had indeed fallen for Edith quickly and deeply, and that she had felt the same way about him.

There are good grounds for suspecting that Wilson may have been an adulterer, however – at the very least in his heart, as Jimmy Carter would put it later. In 1909, when he'd been President of Princeton University and thinking about campaigning for the Governorship of New Jersey, he'd come to know Mary Allen Hulbert, a wealthy hostess with a big house in the state. Some 200 intimate letters were later to come to light, written by the man who was at that time the President: they make a nonsense of the idea that he was some sort of cold-fish scholar. Intense as they are, though, they leave unclear the question of whether what was clearly an 'emotional affair' was ever consummated. The evidence is circumstantial, nothing more.

That this is the case says much for the loyalty and integrity of Mary Hulbert Peck, the woman who may well have kissed but wouldn't tell. This despite lavish offers from Wilson's Republican opponents – up to $300,000 ($8 million today), it's believed – if she'd only hand over the love letters she'd received. And at a time when, having married and divorced since her affair with the President, she was seriously down on her luck and short of cash.

WARREN G. HARDING, 1921–3

If there were to be a Mount Rushmore of scandalous Presidents, Warren G. Harding's head would have to be there. Like Ulysses S. Grant before him, he presided over an age of rampant corruption, though at least arguably not actively corrupt himself. Sure, he couldn't keep it in his pants: his campaign team had been haunted by the fear that one mistress, Carrie Phillips, would decide to tell all. Though they bought her silence for $20,000 ($240,000 today), they could never be sure they wouldn't be outbid. A real looker, she threatened to be a teller too. Ironically, Carrie had been a good friend of Florence, Senator Warren Harding's wife, when they'd met. She and her husband had been on vacation with the Hardings several times while their affair went on. So smitten had the Senator been with Carrie's charms that he'd even been moved to poetry:

Literature's loss was politics'… well, whether politics can really be said to have 'gained' from Harding's career must be doubtful. He himself said, rather plaintively, during his Presidency, 'I am not fit

> By no means all of Senator Harding's affairs had been with his wife's friends. There had been at least one other long-term association, with Grace Cross, a typist from his office.

Warren Harding wags a peremptory finger. He may look commanding, but unfortunately he was unable to establish any real presidential authority over the clique of cronies he had installed in his White House.

for this office and never should have been here.'

He'd actually made something of a habit of involving himself adulterously with Florence's friends. Three years into their marriage, he'd had an affair with Susie Hodder, her till then inseparable companion from childhood. A daughter had been born of this liaison. Florence seems to have decided to grit her teeth and accept her husband's strayings as the price of power as a political wife. Even so, she was furious at her subsequent betrayal by Carrie Phillips.

By no means all of Senator Harding's affairs had been with his wife's friends. There had been at least one other long-term association, with Grace Cross, a typist from his office. Harding is said to have had an assignation with her in the Willard Hotel the night before his inauguration. The fun and games continued throughtout his Presidency: a certain Rosa Hoyle bore him an illegitimate son, whilst Augusta Cole's child by him was terminated. The *Washington Post* proprietor Ned McLean was a good friend and willing panderer: he introduced the President to the ex-chorus girls Maize Haywood and Blossom Jones, as well as a *Post* employee known only as 'Miss Allicott'. When, in 1923, Harding was suddenly taken ill and died, all the indications are that this was the result of food-poisoning. But it's hardly surprising that many Americans suspected that the President's food had been poisoned on purpose; that Florence had snapped after one infidelity too many.

'My Goddamned Friends'

'It's a good thing I'm not a woman,' President Harding confessed at one point. 'I would always be pregnant. I can't say no.' He was always claiming to be helpless: how far this was just a pose, a way of excusing his transgressions to himself, we can't be sure. But easy as he evidently found it to sway women to his will, this great seducer does seem to have found it harder to stand up to men. Or, rather, to *some* men: the ones he was supposed to be closest to, many of them cronies from his home state of Ohio. It wasn't

Florence Harding, nominally First Lady but actually well at the back of a long line of women in Warren Harding's life. The President's sexual incontinence was abject: 'I can't say no,' he lamented.

poker parties that went on till dawn – this despite the fact that Prohibition was supposed to be in force. There was no legal way of getting such supplies, of course, but Harding was on easy terms with important bootleggers: they were hardly that much gamier than his other friends. Together, they were pretty much making a market stall of the government and selling America off to the highest bidder.

A Key Culprit

Albert B. Fall was one of the key culprits: a less suitable candidate for the office of Secretary of the Interior it would have been hard to find. He saw his appointment as an invitation to steal and plunder. Harry M. Daugherty's appointment as Attorney General might have made a good satirical joke if it hadn't been completely serious. As Harding's campaign manager, this Ohio lawyer had predicted with uncanny accuracy many weeks before that deadlock between his man's main rivals would let him through to the nomination. In office, the nation's senior lawyer appears to have also been embezzler-in-chief. He did for his own and his boss's reputation, though, when, called to trial after Harding's death, he 'took the Fifth'.

his enemies he found hard to deal with, he confided. 'My friends, my goddamned friends, they're the ones who keep me walking the floor at nights!'

How much time he spent walking the floor at nights is open to question. As we've seen, he had his hands full with his various amorous encounters. And then there was the time he spent with his friends themselves. Whiskey flowed freely at White House

For sheer, brass-necked boldness in crime, though, there's really no matching the machinations of another member of the 'Ohio Gang', Charles R. Forbes. Though he himself had deserted from the Army, he'd awarded himself the rank of Colonel. Harding placed him at the head of the Veterans' Bureau. Thinking better of it, he forced his director to resign at the beginning of 1923, but not before Forbes had had the chance to steal quarter of a billion dollars. Diverting medical supplies to private dealers for personal profit – and taking kickbacks for the construction of veterans' hospitals – he'd enriched himself beyond the dreams of avarice at the taxpayer's expense.

'THE PRESIDENT'S DAUGHTER'

It was with Nan Britton that the President had his most notorious extra-marital relationship, however: she even wrote a tell-all memoir about it, *The President's Daughter* (1927). In excruciating detail, she describes her erotic encounters with the great man, first in his Senate office and then later in the White House, in at least one case in the closet of the Oval Office. We've grown used to this sort of thing, but on first publication Nan's book caused a positive sensation. Nothing like it had never been seen – or read – before. She and Harding had carried on their affair with the full connivance of his staff and bodyguards – though on one occasion Florence had heard that a tryst was under way and had come rushing down to confront her husband and his other woman. The eponymous daughter, Elizabeth Ann, had been born as early as 1919: she was adopted by Nan's eventual husband some years later.

Nan Britton with Elizabeth Ann – the 'President's Daughter', as Nan claimed in a memoir of that name. No one doubts that she and Warren Harding had a lengthy (and extraordinarily indiscreet) affair.

The Teapot Dome Scandal

The Teapot Dome was (and is) an oilfield in Wyoming. It took its name from an oddly shaped outcrop, the Teapot Rock. As of 1921, it was one of several American fields which had been reserved by a far-sighted President Taft for use by the US Navy in times of emergency. At this point, though, Albert B. Fall took up office as Secretary of the Interior in 1921; within weeks, he'd persuaded President Harding to transfer the administration of these fields to his department. Barely pausing for breath, he promptly offered his friend Edward L. Doheny a lease on one field, at Elk Hills, California, while the Teapot Dome went to another crony, Harry F. Sinclair of Sinclair Oil. Neither concession had gone out to competitive bidding; both the buyers had clearly bought themselves bargains – and both, it turned out, had given Fall generous gifts and 'loans' amounting in total to something like $400,000 ($4.8 million today).

The *Wall Street Journal* was on to the story by 1922, but Harding's government showed no great haste to investigate. Even when proceedings did grind into gear, the way was obscured by the disappearance of documents. Only after Harding's departure from office did real progress start. In 1927, the deals were pronounced unlawful and Albert B. Fall was even sent to prison: the first member of a Presidential cabinet to be jailed for a crime committed while in office.

All Implicated

Though it's often been said that we get the government we deserve, it's hard to think at first what Americans could have done to merit Harding and his kleptomaniac crowd. On closer consideration, though, it's clear that voters and big business alike had been

The Ohio Gang held their meetings in this, the 'Little Green House' on K Street, Washington DC. It was here that they cooked up their various scams – most notoriously, their plans for the Teapot Dome.

This image pokes fun at the Teapot Dome scandal. One positive factor to come out of the situation was that it revealed the problem of natural resource scarcity and the need to protect for the future against the depletion of resources.

looking for an easier time themselves when they'd elected him, on the ticket (dreamed up for him by Albert B. Fall) of 'a return to normalcy'. Lightly coded, this had clearly meant laxness: after the tough discipline of the Taft and Wilson eras, it was hinted, things would ease. There'd be attractive tax-breaks for the wealthy; increased tariffs to cushion industry from foreign competition; a blind eye turned to trusts; and restrictions on immigration to appease the labour unions, which feared the downward pressure incomers put on wages. All gain, no pain, then: a something-for-nothing revolution for America. Is it really so surprising that it ended in tears?

VII

DEPRESSION AND WAR: THE GREAT DECEIVERS

From boom to bust and back to prosperity by way of a world war, the second quarter of the twentieth century was a roller-coaster ride. More vital than ever, as one crisis succeeded another, the US Presidency was at the centre of it all.

◆

'If you don't say anything, you won't be called on to repeat it.'

The 1920s rushed by in a headlong spree: this was the 'Jazz Age', a time of dancing and (despite Prohibition) drink. Americans were in a party mood after the austerities of the Taft–Wilson era and the anxieties of war: there was money to spend; and there were things to spend it on. New technologies, like radio and the movies, had introduced a new kind of consumerism, led by advertising and novel ways of buying, like hire-purchase. Household appliances, from refrigerators

Calvin Coolidge's austere demeanour (left) contrasted with the spirit (both senses) of the 'Roaring Twenties'. But he had his jauntier moments (above); economically speaking, moreover, he was easy-going, believing in _laissez-faire_.

to vacuum cleaners, were available on easy terms. In 1920, there'd been eight million automobiles in the United States; by 1929, there were 18 million. Halfway through the decade, in 1925, 10,000 Model T Fords had been coming off the production line per *day*. Warren Harding had already introduced the idea that the duty of government was to get out of the way, and let the corporations build prosperity. 'The business of America is business,' Calvin Coolidge said, as industrial production rose by some 40 per cent. As the 1920s roared, so the stock-market soared: share-ownership was for ordinary people, who were buying into America's prosperity in unprecedented numbers.

CALVIN COOLIDGE, 1923–9

When Calvin Coolidge came to office, the Presidency was in the throes of a Harding hangover like that of someone who'd downed a bottle or five of bathtub

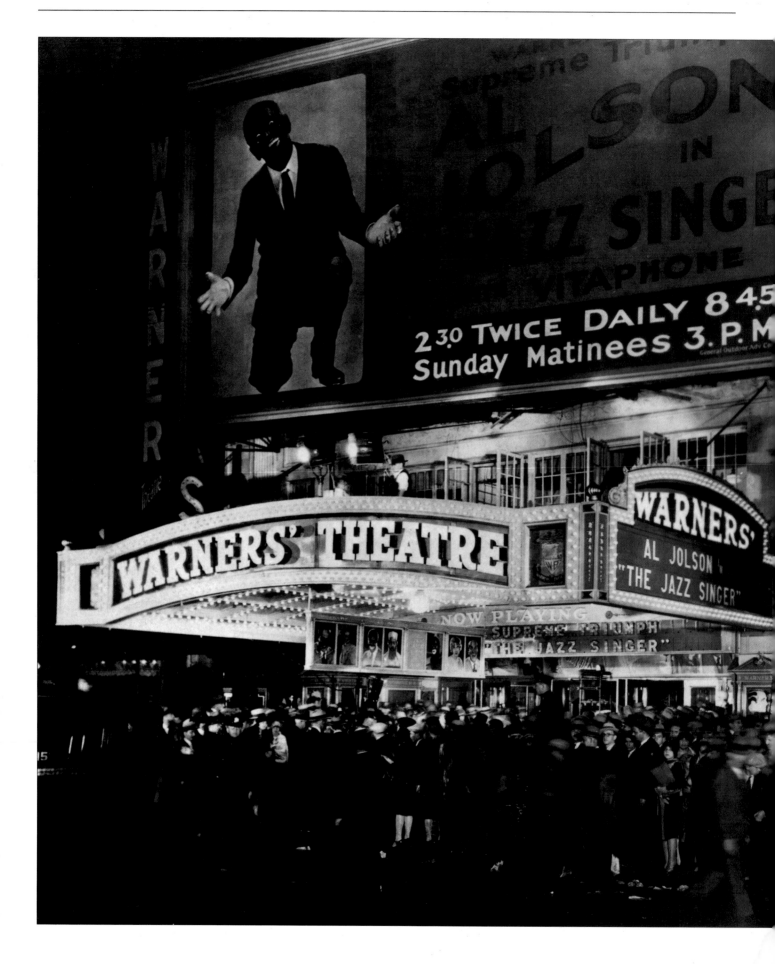

gin. But the conspicuously upright New England lawyer couldn't have been more self-evidently sober. He'd give the country a much-needed dose of rectitude. The beauty of his administration, though, as far as a freewheeling and free-spending America was concerned, was that it would offer the appearance of a return to probity and discipline, whilst not actually tightening any rules. This was, of course, in keeping

> To a slightly disturbing extent at times: it was no real thanks to the President that the prosecution of the Teapot Dome Scandal was finally pursued to its conclusion, or the investigation of other scandals left over from the Harding era.

with Coolidge's *laissez-faire* philosophy: he believed that, as far as possible, the government should leave business to get on with what it did best. But it went much further. Temperamentally, 'Cautious Cal' – so-called from his tardiness in deploying state troopers in the Boston Police Strike of 1919, when he'd been Governor of Massachusetts – was reluctant to intervene in anything, it seemed.

To a slightly disturbing extent at times: it was no real thanks to the President that the prosecution of the Teapot Dome Scandal was finally pursued to its conclusion, or the investigation of other scandals left over from the Harding era. Whilst, in a very vague and general sort of way, he lent his office an air of respectable propriety, he showed little interest in taking any decisive action. It was the same with civil rights: he spoke up for those of African-Americans, deploring the spate of lynchings then going on in the Deep South. Here too, however, he shrank from taking direct action, anxious not to antagonize southern whites. Even when goaded to by Southern Democrat opponents – and begged to by Northern liberals – he refused to take direct action against the

The economic success of the years following World War I underwrote a decade-long spree of jazz and partying (despite Prohibition), of mass-entertainment, of investor-confidence and consumer-boom.

Ellis Island in New York harbour was still a gateway to a new life in the New World for thousands of immigrants each year: thanks to new legislation, though, they were increasingly of Anglo-Saxon origin.

Ku Klux Klan. Typically, he preferred to act quietly: meeting with African-American leaders, as well as Jews and Catholics, who had also been targeted by the bigots of the Klan. Compared with his Presidential predecessors, Coolidge was a pillar of decency in this regard, but his instincts were always not to rock the boat.

That meant a tough line on new immigrants. Over the 1920s as a whole, the US population rose from 105 million to 122 million. Unemployment stayed static – and comparatively low, at around about the million mark, but Americans still viewed incomers with suspicion. In 1924, the Coolidge administration responded to this unwelcoming mood with a crackdown and new quota. Only two per cent of the total number of each nationality already present in the country would be admitted. This, of course, sent out the right message of intolerance to the Anglo-Saxons who still constituted the vast majority of the population – and whose brothers and sisters could still come in pretty much at will. But other ethnic groups felt the door swinging slowly shut: under the quota only 3000 French, 5000 Italian and 25,000 German immigrants would be admitted each year, whilst the merest handful were allowed in from Asia and elsewhere. Those Chinese people already in the country were barred from marrying, as a way of bearing down on the number of new births.

Cold Comfort

But if Coolidge had been loath to intervene to check the headlong expansion of industry and consumerism, he was no more willing to intervene when times turned tough. Whilst the economy continued in its giddy growth, there were already signs of weakness

RACE AND SCIENCE

WAS COOLIDGE A RACIST? Quite literally, the answer has to be yes. Up to a point at least he bought into some of the racial theories of his day. Hence his suggestion that 'Biological laws show us that the Nordic races deteriorate when mixed with other races.' From today's point of view we'd want to ask what these 'biological laws' were and what a 'Nordic race' was – let alone how 'deterioration' was to be measured. All that can be said in the President's favour is that this sort of scientific-sounding nonsense was being spouted at the time by educated people both in North America and Europe. There, of course, it was eventually to result in the horrors of Hitler's 'Final Solution', but when we focus too immediately on this we easily miss the extent to which more 'moderate' versions of this thinking had taken hold.

But Coolidge was a political pragmatist, less interested in 'biological laws' than those of America; for society's sake, he believed, everybody should get on. He aspired to a 'colour blind' view, however unrealistic this may now seem. He certainly talked the talk. Told that Arthur Brooks, his White House butler, was a 'fine colored gentleman', the President replied: 'Brooks is not a colored gentleman. He is a gentleman.'

The white establishment took at best a patronizing view of African Americans. Many officials, politicians and opinion-formers still subscribed to 'scientific' theories which took their inferiority as read.

emerging, writing on the wall for those prepared to read. Not everyone was reaping the benefits of the boom. US agriculture, carried away by its apparent success, had been overproducing for several years: soon the inevitable happened, and produce prices slumped. Tenant farmers in the Midwest struggled to pay their rents; many proprietors had taken out costly mortgages they couldn't now service: the National Farm Bureau sent a deputation to the White House. Sorry, came the response from a polite but apparently indifferent President Calvin Coolidge. It isn't a government matter; I can't help.

Lack of Intervention

The administration's response to growing industrial unrest was not just indifferent but disingenuous. Coolidge had always refused to intervene to regulate pay, conditions and safety standards. And when

For those with eyes to see, the writing was on the wall for the American economy well before the 'Crash': but the breadlines in the slums were out of sight and out of mind for the comfortable classes.

employers imposed restrictive contracts barring union membership, staged lockouts or brought in armed thugs to attack strikers, the government didn't make even the slightest attempt to discourage them. If the workers for a moment looked like winning, however, Coolidge couldn't have been quicker to intervene. When violence flared following a walkout by miners in 1922, his government invoked a wartime law protecting coal production and declared the strike illegal. A strike by 300,000 steelworkers was broken when Coolidge sent in the National Guard to protect blacklegs and suppress demonstrations. Union leaders were arrested on dubious public order charges.

HERBERT HOOVER, 1929–33

For white, middle-class Americans, though, the good times continued through the decade. When it came to the election of 1928, it was 'no contest'. Though Coolidge had refused to run, he had a respected successor in Herbert Hoover, who as Secretary of Commerce could claim to have helped create the economic boom. The debts were soon to come due, however. It's now been largely forgotten, but shares on Wall Street suddenly slumped by 30 per cent in March 1929, a matter of weeks after Hoover's swearing-in as President. They quickly recovered, though and, despite further falterings at the start of September, the mood was buoyant: talk of a collapse was contemptuously dismissed.

On 21 October, however, six million shares were sold, with prices plunging through the floor. Two days later, 13 million shares changed hands. Massive sums were wiped off the value of the most prestigious companies. Losses topped America's total expenditure for the whole of World War I. The banks rallied round, clubbing together and committing to an offer of $30 million to support the stock market, but confidence was gone, and it seemed a drop in the ocean now. On 29 October, no fewer than 5000 banks declared themselves bankrupt. Nine million accounts were wiped out just like that. To this day, the 'Crash' mythology focuses on frantic brokers hurling themselves from Wall Street windows – which didn't happen. The reality was very different: small-town shopkeepers and schoolteachers seeing their savings disappear.

Uncaring?

Hoover was no crook, though there'd been suggestions that his campaign had received contributions from Cuban sugar interests in return for advance information on tariff levels. He was so far from being on the take himself, however, that he'd committed to donate his Presidential salary to charity. But like many moral people, his view was rather blinkered.

His handling of the developing situation was inept, to say the least, though he was to some extent a prisoner of ideology. Like Coolidge, he believed it was the duty of government to create the regulatory conditions in which the economy could run itself; anything more was to be regarded as dangerous

Hoover was not the greatest of communicators, but even he found himself able to use the new technology for wireless broadcasting: the media revolution was about to transform American political life.

Hoover grossly underestimated the scale of the crisis, and completely misjudged the mood of the nation. He had desperate World War I veterans treated as troublemakers when they protested against his inaction.

meddling. It's credibly claimed that he had privately fretted about the overheating in the economy, and even that he'd spoken to bankers, asking them to cut back on the quick no-questions-asked credit that had been doing so much to fuel the speculation, but a public intervention would not have been his way.

Neither was he capable of telling his countrymen (as President Clinton later would): 'I feel your pain.' On the contrary, he told them that things really weren't so bad. This despite the fact that millions had lost their savings and many thousands their jobs and homes. Shanty-towns, or 'Hoovervilles', had sprung up around all America's main cities, and many were forced to sleep under 'Hoover blankets' – old newspapers. 'Nobody is actually starving,' he said, and while this was technically true (few did starve, and they were generally individuals who were vulnerable for other reasons), many thousands were suffering hunger and malnutrition. With a lamentable lack of judgement, he backed plans to provide feed for livestock but obstructed plans to offer assistance to the human hungry, giving rise to the complaint that he cared more for animals than people. It wasn't quite that simple, of course. Handouts would rob men and women of enterprise; they had to have an incentive to keep looking for work, he reasoned – though there was quite clearly no work for the vast majority of them to find.

He was fatuously over-optimistic, telling a 1930 delegation which had come to ask for the setting up of federal aid programmes: 'Gentlemen, you have come sixty days too late. The Depression is over.' If only this had been true. The Great Depression had yet to tighten its grip on the United States and the world: it was to leave its scars on an entire generation. But Hoover seems to have been in deep denial, persuading himself that the 'Bonus Army' of unemployed World War I veterans who in 1932 turned up in Washington with their families in desperate shape were nothing more than troublemakers, who needed to be dealt with firmly. As though they were the real army of an enemy power, he dispatched armed troops with machine-guns and tanks to see them off. They were

led by General Douglas MacArthur, later to take charge of the occupation of Japan: two veterans were killed in the squalid mayhem that ensued.

The rural poor and landless flocked to the cities in search of some work. But, as often as not, they ended up in dismal shantytowns – 'Hoovervilles'. This one was in the outskirts of Seattle.

Southern Stratagems

Hoover, though identified with Coolidge's non-interventionist attitudes, had built up a real reputation as humanitarian. In the aftermath of World War I, he'd organized relief for a hungry Europe. Defeated Germany wasn't excluded; nor was Bolshevik Russia. He'd had something of a halo when he entered government, then, though this had been badly tarnished by his handling of the Great Mississippi Flood of 1927. In keeping with administration thinking, he practised a sort of non-interventionist

intervention: rather than deploying troops or National Guardsmen, he got 'Main Street' to respond.

And it was all a great success, local businessmen and pastors coming together with town officials to organize assistance for thousands of families made homeless by the flood. But being local businessmen, pastors and town officials in the Deep South in the 1920s, they wouldn't have dreamt of treating African-Americans on an equal footing. White families were first in line for assistance; aid was given to white landlords rather than black sharecroppers; African-Americans were herded into camps and then brutally beaten if they tried to leave. And, in a system that offered a profoundly unpleasant reminder of the days of slavery, black labour was conscripted into work-gangs to be bawled at hours at a time by white overseers.

Too late, Hoover appreciated his error. In hopes of securing the African-American vote for the forthcoming elections, he promised community leaders concessions if they'd keep quiet about what had happened. They grudgingly agreed, only to find that things had moved on in Hoover's political calculations. With the White vote looking soft in the South, he'd introduced the so-called 'Southern

Much of the sugar grown on Cuban plantations like this one was gobbled up directly by a voracious US market. Hoover's 1928 campaign had run into controversy over payments from producers.

> In hopes of securing the African-American vote for the forthcoming elections, he promised community leaders concessions if they'd keep quiet about what had happened. They grudgingly agreed.

Strategy': basically, brutally, this involved pandering to racism in the South by ditching African-American leaders at local level and appointing white men in their place. African-Americans realized too late what was happening, so Hoover was able to have his electoral cake and eat it in 1928, winning votes from both black and white voters in the South. They were once bitten, twice shy, however, and their alienation had a significant bearing on Hoover's defeat in 1932.

FRANKLIN D. ROOSEVELT, 1933–45

Franklin Delano Roosevelt's background was about as aristocratic as the American Republic has to offer. He was descended from 'Old Dutch' settlers on his father's side. His mother, Sara Delano, could claim descent from a family of Huguenots (French Protestants forced to leave their native land in the seventeenth century) – the Delanos' original name had been 'de la Noye'. The Roosevelts had for generations been prominent in banking and in trade. It would be wrong to say that they were 'no relation' of Theodore Roosevelt's family, but they weren't anything like as closely related as might be assumed. That was just as well, given that Eleanor Roosevelt was Theodore's niece, and Franklin married her (his fifth cousin, once removed) in 1905. Sara was dead set against the match, but then she was notoriously possessive and domineering: it seems unlikely that any daughter-in-law would have done.

The couple seem to have been happy together, though Eleanor's relationship with her mother-in-law was fraught, and she was quoted as saying that she wasn't wild about sex, 'an ordeal to be endured'. She endured it at least often enough to bear her husband six children (five of whom survived), while he set about carving out a career in politics. In 1910, cashing in on the appeal of his family name in the area in which he'd been brought up (near Hyde Park in the Hudson Valley), he got himself elected to the New York State Senate. He quickly showed his crusading zeal, taking on the Tammany Hall machine which till then had

dominated state politics. At the same time, though, he was building his profile at a national level, being selected by Woodrow Wilson as an Assistant Secretary for the Navy in 1913. This meant his withdrawal from state politics, at least for now.

Newport News

Roosevelt came unstuck at the end of his tenure as Assistant Navy Secretary over the handling of the Newport Sex Scandal. Reports had been received over a period of time about homosexual encounters between sailors at the Rhode Island naval base and (sometimes prominent) members of the local community. There were stories of riotous parties in

A blue-blood in the White House, Franklin D. Roosevelt was to bring a touch of class to American political life – though his domestic arrangements didn't necessarily bear close scrutiny.

which cocaine, cross-dressing and drinking were rife (Prohibition had, of course, just begun), not to mention unlawful sexual acts.

FDR doesn't seem to have been directly involved in the decision as to how the investigation was to be carried out: ultimately, however, he was the man in charge. Those in charge of the inquiry chose to use attractive young men to infiltrate the scene; in the process they participated (apparently willingly) in what went on. A committee of local clergymen, upset that one of their colleagues in the cloth had been 'stung', protested against what they argued had been a process of unfair entrapment. An official inquiry agreed that, since they'd clearly committed offences themselves, the informers' credibility couldn't be relied on. The case collapsed, and Roosevelt was reprimanded.

Infidelity, Illness and Accommodation

It seems to have been the following year that 'FDR' embarked on his first affair, with Eleanor's social secretary, Lucy Mercer. Their relationship continued until, in 1918, Eleanor discovered letters they'd written: upset and outraged, she demanded a divorce. But the anger of a betrayed wife was nothing to that of a disappointed mother, it appeared: if Franklin was divorced, she swore, she would disinherit him entirely. Perhaps reflecting too that divorce for Franklin would, in that age, have also certainly meant the end of his political career, Eleanor took pity on her husband. She agreed to remain married to him, so long as he concluded his affair forthwith. They remained companions but even so, it seems, the trust between

Eleanor Roosevelt's relationship with her husband appears to have been closely companionate, but borderline platonic. She saved her most intense emotions for her friendships with other women – and for her political passions.

them had gone. Increasingly, they saw themselves as separate. They still spent time together, but Eleanor was going her own way emotionally and intellectually: she had interests and political objectives of her own.

The year 1920 saw Franklin selected as Vice-Presidential running-mate to Democratic candidate James M. Cox, but their campaign was swept aside by Warren Harding and Calvin Coolidge's landslide victory. The following year, Roosevelt was felled by an attack of what's thought to have been polio: paralyzed from the waist down, he spent most of his time in a wheelchair from that point on. 'Most' of his time because, convinced that his political ambitions would be threatened if he revealed his weakness, he trained himself to stand up to speak and even to walk short distances, with the help of leg-braces and a stick. To an extent that seems unthinkable today, an obliging media connived in a cover-up which was in its way as scandalous as any other in American political history. Eleanor tended him dutifully, even devotedly, though the nurse–patient relationship established a distance between them which seems to have suited her. (At some deep psychological level, the historian Nigel Hamilton has suggested, she saw his illness as his 'just reward'.)

One enduring result of Roosevelt's Vice-Presidential campaign was his relationship with Marguerite 'Missy' LeHand, who'd come to work with him as private

Lucy Mercer's affair with Franklin D. Roosevelt almost brought his marriage to an end before it had barely begun. Eleanor forgave him – up to a point – but she was never really able to fully trust him again.

secretary at that time. She remained with him for the next 21 years, a fixture in his home – even part of his family. And, it has been said, a second mistress. She certainly played the part of White House hostess when Eleanor wasn't there: this doesn't seem to have been a problem for the First Lady.

What she felt about the fact that Franklin was back in touch with his First Mistress, meanwhile, we have no way of knowing. Lucy Mercer had married a wealthy widower, and was now Mrs Rutherfurd. There seems to be little doubt, though, that she was seeing her old lover again: the only dispute is how often and under what circumstances. The number of their *known* encounters over the following years is fairly small: disabled as he was, it would have been hard for Franklin to get out from under Missy's watchful eye. But some scholars have suggested that outwardly chatty and merely friendly letters between the pair were actually coded communications, designed to set up trysts. What we do know for sure is that theirs was a lasting relationship – and that Eleanor's was an enduring hurt. She was deeply wounded later when she learned that Lucy had been with her husband when he died.

The wheelchair-bound Roosevelt we've come to know from historical photos wouldn't have been recognized by the electors of his own day: he took great pains to disguise the effects of his crippling polio.

'EMN'

ONE AFTERNOON IN THE INDIAN SUMMER of 1924, Eleanor had a picnic on the Roosevelt estate a couple of miles from Springwood, her Hyde Park home, with two friends and fellow activists for women's rights. Marion Dickerman and Nancy Cook were not just political comrades but life-partners – they'd fallen in love when they were at school together in Syracuse. That evening, back at the house with Franklin, they ruefully reflected that this would have to be their last outing of the year. It was the future President's idea that he should sign some land over to the three of them so they could build a little cottage at their favourite picnic-spot: he set the legal formalities in motion there and then. Val-Kill (so-called because it was situated on the banks of Fallkill Creek) became a home for Marion and Nancy, and a weekend retreat and office for Eleanor. Quite what the domestic arrangement was we do not know, but it struck many as odd that the towels were monogrammed with the initials of all three women, 'EMN'. Eleanor had a close and lasting friendship with at least one other lesbian couple: the women's rights campaigners Esther Lape and Elizabeth Read.

ELEANOR AND EARL

THERE DOESN'T SEEM TO BE ANY real doubt that many of Eleanor's feelings were focused on the women in her life, but this doesn't seem to have stopped her from being drawn to men. Her relationship with Earl Miller appears to have been particularly close, the state trooper acted as her bodyguard when Franklin was Governor of New York between 1929 and 1932. Earl was 32 to her 44 when he was assigned to her. Their friendship may have been just that: they shared an interest in sports, including swimming and tennis. But they kept close company in Franklin's frequent absences, and Earl's wife eventually cited Eleanor as the co-respondent in her divorce. It's thought that they wrote one another every day, till she died in 1962, though all these letters appear to have been destroyed.

Earl and Eleanor: a happy couple? Or was theirs no more than a professional bodyguard–client relationship, close but correct? Speculation was rife back then and has scarcely subsided since.

'Hick Darling ...'

A formidable First Lady, Eleanor Roosevelt took very seriously her role as the most prominent woman in the Free World. She used the platform her position gave her to make the case for the advancement of women and the foregrounding of their concerns. And she wasn't talking about recipes or housework. Rather, in her newspaper columns and press conferences (often all-female), she addressed a considerable range of issues, including education, sex discrimination and social welfare. Her feminist views, and the freedom with which she expressed them, inevitably raised conservative hackles and gave rise to rumours: she couldn't be a proper woman,

Lorena Hickok (second from right) got to know Eleanor (right) as a reporter in 1932 and the two women were soon inseparable. Inevitably, it was soon being suggested that they were not just friends but lovers.

that was clear. It's easy enough to imagine that the suggestions of lesbianism might have been based on no more than prejudices of this sort. She wouldn't have been the first or last feminist to suffer from such smears.

But Mrs Roosevelt's relationship with reporter Lorena Hickok was so close, it's hardly surprising that it should have set tongues wagging in Washington. 'Hick', as Eleanor came to call her, had worked closely with the future First Lady, covering her life during the Presidential campaign of 1932 and the early months of her husband's administration. Hickok gave Eleanor a ring, which she even wore to Franklin's inauguration. Mrs Roosevelt refers to it in a letter of 7 March 1933.

> 'I wish I could lie down beside you tonight & take you in my arms,' reads one, the date of which is unknown. Whatever the two women did or didn't get up to when they managed to make time together, it seems clear that they were a little more than 'just good friends'.

Many of the letters the two wrote each other were subsequently destroyed. 'Hick' herself is known to have burned at least 15. But enough have survived to give us pause: 'I wish I could lie down beside you tonight & take you in my arms,' reads one, the date of which is unknown. Whatever the two women did or didn't get up to when they managed to make time together, it seems clear that they were a little more than 'just good friends'.

Rich Pickings

Two great realities overshadowed the whole of Roosevelt's (unprecedented and unrepeated) three-term Presidency: those of the Great Depression and World War II. We've already seen that the massive commitment of mobilizing for war tends to create opportunities for the corrupt. Government is never 'bigger', the contracts never fatter (or more hastily prepared) than they are in times of conflict. FDR's programme for tackling the economic crisis involved investment on a comparable scale. The 'New Deal' involved great and far-reaching projects organized by a bewildering range of different agencies: everything

The raid on Pearl Harbor allowed Franklin D. Roosevelt to override objections to America's entrance into World War II. It's even been suggested that he knew in advance of Japan's 'surprise' attack.

BY EXECUTIVE ORDER

THOUGH NOW NOTORIOUS, Executive Order 9066 went more or less unquestioned when Roosevelt signed it in 1942. It provided for the internment of those with Foreign Enemy Ancestry. About 120,000 men, women and children of Japanese descent were placed in sealed camps until the conclusion of the war. Of these only about 40 per cent were Japanese-born; most were second- or even third-generation Japanese Americans. Approximately 3000 people of Italian descent were locked away, as well as in the region of 11,000 'Germans'. These, ironically, included many Jews, who'd fled from Hitler's Germany only to find themselves rounded up and imprisoned in the United States.

from artists' and writers' projects to vast hydroelectric schemes. The Tennessee Valley Authority (TVA) alone involved the construction of over 20 dams: the opportunities for corruption and theft were mind-boggling. As would be expected, investigations subsequently revealed that huge amounts of money and materials had gone astray – but none of the loot seems to have found its way back to the White House or to central government.

The President's hands appear to have been clean; as do those of all his senior officials. When America entered World War II, it was substantially the same story. Such was the scale and complexity of the war effort that a good deal of abuse was practically inevitable. The surprising thing is how little the higher levels of officialdom and government got involved.

A Way into War?

Most Americans may recall their country's role in World War II with pride, and Roosevelt's leadership through that episode with admiration. Yet, whether or not it can be classed as a scandal, suspicions have surrounded Roosevelt's role in the run-up to the War, with some suggesting that he knew about the attack on Pearl Harbor but failed to act. It's true that the President had been in a minority in America in

wanting the United States to involve itself in the conflict with Hitler's Germany of the outset. While there were undoubtedly some who supported the Nazis – anti-Semitism, Aryan domination and all – more were of German descent and didn't want to see their new homeland at war with the old country, whilst yet more Americans simply felt a war in Europe was not their problem. Roosevelt's view was that Hitler was a threat to freedom, whose militarism had to be resisted. He was eager for America to fight, but knew he could not convince his country.

Hence, the conspiracy theory articulated most famously by Robert Stinnett in the book *Day of Deceit* (1999). This suggests the President turned a blind eye to Japanese preparations, and a deaf ear to intercepted communications. In this analysis, the Pacific Fleet was the bait in the trap which would allow Roosevelt to achieve his objective and get America into the War. Since something like 2500 Americans were killed in the attack, it's a momentous claim.

Challenged Children

Unremarkably, perhaps, given the circumstances of their childhood, the Roosevelts' sons and daughters turned out troubled adults. Between them, the five made no fewer than 19 attempts at marriage. Anna, her father's favourite, seems to have had a difficult relationship with Eleanor, who – it's been alleged –

> Such was the scale and complexity of the war effort that a good deal of abuse was practically inevitable. The surprising thing is how little the higher levels of officialdom and government got involved.

turned a blind eye to her abuse by a series of governesses. This may help explain why Anna appears to have conspired against her mother, assisting as a go-between for Franklin and Lucy Mercer as they continued their affair.

Elliott, the second of Franklin and Eleanor's surviving sons, gave every indication of becoming a credit to his parents. He served with distinction as a reconnaissance pilot in World War II. But he was subsequently called before a Senate subcommittee investigating financial irregularities in the procurement of the Hughes Aircraft Company's D-2 reconnaissance plane, previously turned down as being inferior to a rival Lockheed model. In 1943, it transpired, Elliott and a group of other officers had allowed themselves

In 1932, at the age of just 21, Elliott Roosevelt became the boss of Gilpin Airlines. Some suspected a 'payoff' in return for a father's blind eye to breaches in regulations by the aviation industry.

to be invited out to Hollywood by Howard Hughes, to be wined and dined, and entertained by actresses and night-club hostesses. Young Roosevelt wasn't charged with any crime, but it didn't look too good – especially in light of the fact that the ill-advised expedition had taken place in wartime, when their comrades-at-arms had been risking their lives in North Africa, Europe and the Pacific.

His father was never to hear of this disgrace. He'd died of a stroke on 12 April 1945, just three months into his fourth term and in the final days of World War II.

HARRY S. TRUMAN, 1945–53

Truman arrived in the White House just in time for the honour of being the President who had won victory in Europe – a triumphant moment, yet it can't have seemed so at the time. Before he'd even got his feet under the desk in the Oval Office, he was having to take the decision over whether to drop the atom bombs on Hiroshima and Nagasaki. For some historians, that was an atrocity which consigns Truman to the most dismal depths of any 'dark history' of the US Presidency – over 130,000 died in the blasts, and that was just the start. The number of casualties doubled in the weeks and months that followed. Innocent civilians sickened and wasted away in agonizing and disfiguring ways, longer-term victims of the fallout.

Offset against this, though, has to be the likely cost in casualties – among US and Allied forces and the civilian population of Japan – if Truman hadn't taken the tough decision to drop the bombs. Prior to 6 August 1945, Japan's military rulers had been showing every sign of settling in for a lengthy siege. Even after Hiroshima they showed a marked reluctance to come to terms. It wasn't as if the fighting in the islands had been such a picnic for US soldiers, sailors or airmen (or for indigenous peoples) – or the firestorms in their cities so pleasant for the Japanese.

That still leaves controversial questions: why the second bomb, at Nagasaki on 9 August? Some have suggested that this attack was an opportunist bit of weapons-testing: 'Fat Boy' was a different type of device from Hiroshima's 'Little Boy'. If they hadn't dropped it then, when would they have got the chance

Harry Truman's spectacles were always there as a reminder of how he'd white-lied his way into military service in World War I. Presidents since have been much more dishonest, few have been half as decent.

to use it? Others say that Japan wasn't even the real target in what was the opening salvo of the Cold War: the attacks were intended as a warning to the Soviet Union, already viewed as the enemy for the next decades. In fairness to Truman, he can hardly have had any idea of what the impact of this unprecedented airborne assault was going to be. He himself had warned the Japanese of 'a rain of ruin from the air, the like of which has never been seen on this earth'. It was one thing to say that, though; quite another to appreciate what it was really going to mean.

'To Err is Truman'

It's hard to summon up too much moral outrage about some of Truman's supposed transgressions. Strictly speaking, it was a 'scandal' that he misled recruiters about his age and state of health before World War I, dropping two of his 33 years and memorizing the eyesight-chart. But when so many in history (not excluding US Presidents) are known to have made strenuous efforts to avoid military service in times when it was compulsory, how indignant are we really going to get about a guy who stretched the truth so he could enlist? A model husband, Truman was clearly a conscientious public servant too. He left office with little more than his military pension to see him through. In all obvious respects, then, something of a paragon among presidents: what's the seeker-after-scandal supposed to do?

A HAPPY COUPLE

SOPHISTICATED COMMENTATORS agreed that Bess Truman didn't exactly adorn the position of First Lady. She wasn't a beauty; nor an elegant hostess. In fact she found it wearisome to have to entertain important guests, with all the formality and ceremony that entailed, and was obviously uncomfortable talking to the press. That said, both she and her husband were a huge hit with the White House staff, who loved the easy way the First Couple would talk to them as

Harry Truman's better-half Bess had been the object of his adoration since the age of six. They have to rank among the most devoted couples ever to have occupied the White House.

equals. Servants who opened doors or brought trays of teacups found themselves being introduced to visiting presidents, prime ministers and monarchs, as if that was the most natural thing in the world.

Truman had met Bess Wallace at Sunday school in Independence, Missouri, at the age of six, and had fallen in love with her 'blue eyes' and 'golden curls'. A clichéd tale of childhood sweethearts, then: he seemed too besotted to be true – but true he was. He brusquely cut off the young officer who, after a session at the Potsdam Conference of 1945, offered to fix him up with some female company. 'I married my sweetheart. She doesn't run around on me, and I don't run around on her.'

No need to worry. Truman's reign wasn't the time of perfect probity which might have been expected, even if the President was a passive bystander rather than an active crook. Though in most respects a much better man than Ulysses S. Grant or Warren Harding, he let himself down as they had done by his lack of judgement in making appointments and his refusal to see a good buddy brought down. Like Harding, he came to Washington with a group of friends from his home state. They soon became known as the 'Missouri Gang'.

The Missouri Gang

A President has to start somewhere. As often as not that means state politics, and all too frequently it means a wagonload of baggage. So it was with Truman, who'd risen through the ranks of the Democratic Party in Missouri under the patronage of Tom Pendergast. The Kansas City boss had created an empire of graft and influence, though it had all come tumbling down in 1939, when he was convicted of tax evasion, imprisoned and disgraced. He died in 1945, and Truman caused a stir when, just days after his inauguration, he made time to attend the funeral of a man he still called his 'friend'. But many more 'friends' from the Missouri days found their way into positions of influence in Truman's slipstream: they quickly set about pillaging the government's coffers.

Kansas City lawyer John W. Snyder became Secretary of the Treasury. As such, he had to take overall responsibility for the workings of the Internal Revenue. And that's quite some responsibility to have to take. For within weeks of the Truman administration's arrival on the scene, a

Harry S. Truman completed his army service through the mud, blood and thunder of World War I with the same unswerving commitment and conscientiousness he was to show so many years later in the presidency.

> No one has suggested that the President himself was involved, but he was undoubtedly culpably incurious. Not until Truman had left office did these arrangements finally come under investigation.

culture of corruption had become firmly entrenched. Politically appointed chiefs within the Bureau were enriching themselves by accepting bribes to turn a blind eye to tax-evasions, or by blackmailing those they'd caught trying to escape their liabilities. No one has suggested that the President himself was involved, but he was undoubtedly culpably incurious. Not until Truman had left office did these arrangements finally come under investigation: 166 officials were dismissed.

Cedar County lawyer Donald Dawson was the President's political adviser. He was also a director of the Reconstruction Finance Corporation (RFC), set up by Herbert Hoover in the early days of the Great Depression. It was there to help jump-start job-creating ventures by important companies. But Dawson used his position in the RFC to arrange generous loans to businessmen friends without collateral, receiving expensive gifts and favours in return. Truman just wouldn't be told: when rumours of what was happening caused a scandal, he threw his full Presidential weight behind his Missouri friend.

Another Missouri man, Major General Harry H. Vaughan, was Truman's trusted Military Aide. He embarrassed his boss by soliciting gifts of consumer-goods on his behalf, as well as on his own. It was becoming the norm to accept gifts and 'freebies', from anything like fur

Too pure a president can be as problematic as a dishonest one. Truman remained oblivious while his Treasury Secretary J.W. Snyder (seen with him, left) turned the US administration into a den of corruption.

coats to holidays. More serious was Vaughan's subsequently uncovered role as the most senior of the 'Five Percenters' – government officials who'd offered access and assistance to contractors on a commission basis.

Edwin W. Pauley was actually from Indiana, but he was right at home with the ways of the 'Missouri Gang'. A powerful oilman, the President had appointed him Undersecretary to the Navy – a huge consumer of petroleum. As the historian Thomas A. Bailey has said, this was a 'classic case of the wolf

being asked to guard the sheep'. Far from fighting for justice, Attorney General J. Howard McGrath appeared to be more interested in guarding the government's back: he had to resign in 1952 when it emerged that he had intervened to shut down an investigation being conducted by his own department. As ever, Truman doesn't seem to have been involved; still less did he benefit financially from any of these goings-on, but hadn't it been he who'd famously said 'The buck stops here'?

Junky Joe

It was during Truman's term that Joseph McCarthy's witchhunt against 'Reds' began. The President has been criticized for not having done enough to stop him. Truman appears to have found McCarthy's campaign

distasteful and disturbing but to have felt unable to act for fear of seeming soft on Communism himself.

In hindsight, though, it does seem as though the Truman administration may have been more timid than it needed to be. McCarthy was a proven liar and a fraud. Though 'Tail-Gunner Joe' had indeed been in active combat, he lied about the length of his service and the number of missions he'd flown. He'd also forged an official letter of commendation, supposedly signed by Admiral Chester W. Nimitz, and claimed an accidental injury was a 'war wound'. He was wildly inconsistent and patently unreliable even in his accusations against Communists. Truman and his staff leaned over backwards to accommodate him, though, to the extent of helping him cover up his heroin addiction.

McCarthy's early political career was shaped to some extent by his background in Wisconsin, a state with a large population of German-Americans. He first came to prominence in 1946, calling for 'fair treatment' for 84 SS-men on trial at Dachau for massacring American prisoners of war. His forgiving attitude toward Nazis certainly wasn't extended to the Communists, real and imagined, who he claimed were 'infesting' US official and cultural life. His drive against 'Reds Under the Bed' began in 1950: it swept through America's great institutions – from the Army to Hollywood – cutting off important careers and creating a climate of fear and paralysis. Moreover, many observers noticed how close anti-Communism came to anti-Semitism: a high proportion of those branded as subversives were also Jews. So close did these criticisms come to home that McCarthy felt compelled to deflect them by taking on a Jew, Roy Cohn, as his right-hand man.

In parallel with the 'Red Peril', McCarthy whipped up the so-called 'Lavender Scare' – the suggestion that homosexuals were 'taking over' official life. Ironically, it was an 'open secret' among Milwaukee's gay community that Senator McCarthy was homosexual: it was said that he himself joked he dated girls only as 'window dressing'. Roy Cohn, barely closeted, recruited his own lover to work with him in his office.

Joe McCarthy unmasks some more guilty men: hypocritical as its origins were, the Wisconsin senator's reign of fear and suspicion cast a deep, dark shadow over the America of the 1950s.

DWIGHT D. EISENHOWER, 1953–61

The post-war peace never got started. The dust and smoke of World War II cleared only to reveal two rival power-blocs locked into a bitter Cold War. The military virtues seemed as appropriate as ever to the man who was going to have to lead the Free World against the forces of Communism: who embodied them more perfectly than the man who had been Supreme Allied Commander in Europe in the conflict just gone by? 'I like Ike' said the campaign-slogan; and it seemed to be a sentiment the American people shared. He was swept home by a landslide in the elections of 1952.

And, in fairness, they hadn't been misled. What you saw in Eisenhower was pretty much what you got. He was a plain-dealer; an honest-to-goodness soldier with a sense of duty and a well-developed flair for leadership. He was very much a man of his times, however, and many of what may now seem more questionable decisions on his part were the pretty-much-inevitable consequences of Cold War thinking. Truman felt angry that Eisenhower had ducked a confrontation with Joseph McCarthy – and it's true that as a war hero he would have been uniquely placed to call the great bully's bluff. Eisenhower's reluctance to get 'into the gutter' with the Wisconsin Senator is understandable, though; Truman had hardly acquitted himself with great courage in this regard.

It's true that Eisenhower presided over an unprecedented militarization of America during the 1950s (even the Interstate highway system was part of this rearmament scheme), but America had committed itself totally to the 'arms race'

Left: Tried in the fire of war, Dwight D. Eisenhower proved to be a strong but peace-loving leader: it was he who first denounced the emergence of the 'military-industrial complex'.

Right: General Eisenhower gives the order of the day. As Supreme Commander of Allied Forces in Europe during World War II, the future president had the toughest possible preparation for high office.

> The confrontation with the Soviet Union was the overwhelming reality of his Presidency; the opposition between the two superpowers the overarching structure that defined the post-war order.

by this time. The confrontation with the Soviet Union was the overwhelming reality of his Presidency; the opposition between the two superpowers the overarching structure that defined the post-war order. The President was something of a sceptic, in fact: it was he who identified the emergence of a 'military-industrial complex' – in which the arms industry, the military and government were locked into a mutually

Mamie Eisenhower was surely not the only wife who found her husband returning from the war a changed man, different in his thoughts and affections. They'd arguably been ill-suited from the start.

supporting and mutually perpetuating relationship. He feared that the diversion of so many resources into the defence of the NATO countries of America and Europe risked destroying 'from within what we are trying to defend from without'.

Mamie and Kay (and Gladys)

Cheerful, friendly, feminine, Mamie Eisenhower made an extremely popular First Lady. A pity she wasn't quite so popular with her husband. She hadn't been his first love: that honour belonged to Gladys Harding, a girl from Abilene, Kansas. Having bombarded her with romantic letters while he was away at West Point Military Academy, he'd asked her to marry him when he graduated in 1915. She'd put him off, though: her doting father didn't think the future President good enough, while she herself was envisaging a future as a concert pianist. Marriage simply didn't fit into her plans just now.

Dwight got the message. Posted to San Antonio, Texas, he met Mamie Doud within weeks. The daughter of a meat-packing millionaire, Mamie was rich and pretty, lively and vivacious – she didn't take herself as seriously as Gladys had. It was love at first sight – and they married in some haste, in July 1916, though Eisenhower at least was to repent at leisure. Mamie was bubbly and attractive, but she wasn't exactly laden down with 'depth'. She was great fun, but didn't have Dwight's more serious side. When it

came to the longer term, they didn't have all that much in common.

It was no great surprise, then, that far from home and in the adrenaline-rush of war, he should have fallen for his driver in London, Kay Summersby. An ex-model of Anglo-Irish parentage, she'd already acquired a degree of notoriety: she was being cited as the co-respondent in a divorce case when she was assigned to Eisenhower. That they became close isn't really in doubt, though how far they got is disputed. Some say it was an 'emotional affair'. Kay herself, in a later memoir, claimed that they'd a couple of times got to the point of making love, but that the General hadn't been able to perform. While some have scoffed, it isn't necessarily so improbable that he should have been impotent when things got to this point. Eisenhower's sense of duty was strong – and so, accordingly, was the guilt he felt toward Mamie, whom he'd married, however much he might have come to regret that fact.

We owe to – of all people – President Truman the revelation that 'Ike' at one point seriously contemplated divorcing Mamie so he could wed Kay. Eisenhower wrote to him from Europe, asking his advice. But he'd chosen the wrong confidant in the ultra-married Truman, who wrote back and told him that he'd have him cashiered from the service if he so

Eisenhower's relationship with Kay Summersby, his wartime driver, was forged in a shared experience of the dangers and the stresses of war: deep as it was, though, their affair seems not to have been sexual.

much thought of embarking on such a course. His last act as President, Truman said, had been to get hold of Eisenhower's army file and destroy his letters for the general's own protection.

Cold War Compromises

A generation earlier, Franklin D. Roosevelt was said to have remarked about the Nicaraguan dictator Anastasio Somoza: 'He may be a son of a bitch, but he's our son of a bitch.' There's no doubt that the Cold War brought some strange bedfellows for America. One of Eisenhower's first actions as President, for example, was to cosy up with Spain's Fascist dictator Francisco Franco. By signing the Pact of Madrid with him in 1953, he brought a murderous pariah in out of the cold. That same year, the CIA helped to topple Iran's democratically elected Prime Minister Mohammed Mossadeq, fearful that his plans to nationalize the country's oil industry would harm Western interests. America preferred the Shah – a tyrant and a torturer. The action sowed the seeds of a distrust between Iran and America which has continued to this day. It was the same story in Central America: in Guatemala, Jacobo Arbenz's popular government was toppled with the assistance of US intelligence because of its stated intention of breaking the power of the United Fruit Company and the landowning elite.

As the old European colonies in Africa and Asia rose up and won their independence, the US and Soviet superpowers fought for influence: a period of 'proxy wars' was the result. In the Congo, Patrice Lumumba commanded popular support – but also the favour of the Soviets. He was abducted and assassinated – it's believed with US help. His replacement, Joseph Mobutu, plundered his country on an epic scale, but was reliable in his allegiance to the West. In Southeast Asia, Ho Chi Minh had led Vietnam to freedom from French colonial rule, his heroic struggle winning him a great deal of moral authority among his countrymen and -women: Eisenhower acknowledged that in a free election he would have won 80 per cent of the popular vote.

He might have been a hit with his Iranian countrymen, but Mossadeq didn't please US oil-interests, so he had to go. Increasingly, America was making the political weather in countries around the world.

(He himself had won 57 per cent, in what was classed as a 'landslide'.) But his Communist sympathies barred him, as far as the United States were concerned. America helped Ngo Dinh Diem to set up his own Republic of Vietnam in the south of the peninsula, and looked the other way while he terrorized the Vietnamese people.

Red Faces Over Russia

American superiority in military technology was clear, though it was denied by the Soviets, of course – and, it's often been alleged, by an American military-industrial complex, which had an interest in keeping Americans in fear. In 1960, however, the Soviets scored a rare coup when they succeeded in shooting down a U2 spyplane over Russia. The U2 flew so high that it was out of reach of fighter planes – and,

As democratically elected President of Guatemala, Jacobo Arbenz had sworn to break the hold of the United Fruit Company: the CIA didn't wait to hear more, but backed a coup that broke him first.

generally, of surface-to-air missiles – but this one was caught by a lucky shot from a battery in the Ural Mountains. The Americans, realizing that their plane was lost, came out with a cock-and-bull story about it having been a NASA research plane flying over Turkey whose pilot's oxygen supply had failed. They even painted a U2 to look like a NASA aircraft, only to find that the actual plane had survived and the Soviets were showing pictures to the world's press.

Finding themselves in a hole, they kept digging. A new story was now released. It had been a NASA plane – Washington was still sure of that – and flying

A GAME OF DOMINOES

IT WAS EISENHOWER WHO, at a press conference in 1954, first publicly propounded the so-called 'Domino Theory'. Third World countries, as they were then called (the first two worlds were the industrialized West and the 'Iron Curtain' countries of the Communist East) were like a row of dominoes standing up on their ends in line. When you pushed on the first domino, it fell against the next one, which in turn tipped over into the next one, which toppled the next – and so it went on in a continuous rippling wave. It was the same with Communism, Eisenhower argued: as the left came to power in one country, their comrades in

neighbouring states were emboldened to take power in their own. This 'falling domino' effect had to be stopped at any cost.

The 'Domino Theory' isn't as absurd as is often claimed. There's no doubt that revolutionaries in one country are likely to be encouraged by the success of those they see as their brothers and sisters in another. Suddenly, what seemed like idealistic pipe-dreams appear to be realistic. Unfortunately for the United States, the converse of the theory was also true. American-backed oppression in one country bred resistance to American-backed governments elsewhere.

over Turkey, innocently monitoring the weather, before the oxygen system had failed. But it did seem possible, they admitted, that it might have drifted north and come down in the USSR. It was at this point that the Soviets produced their trump card. Till now, they'd kept quiet about the fact that pilot Gary Powers had successfully baled out and drifted down to earth. The Americans had assumed he must be dead. His plane had been found as well, and its specialized surveillance equipment recovered. To Eisenhower's intense embarrassment, Powers was paraded on TV. There was no way the nature of his mission could be concealed: their efforts up to now simply looked silly. America and its President had been caught in a flat-out lie.

The 'Invasion of Arkansas'
'They are not bad people,' said Eisenhower to his Chief Justice Earl Warren, of the Southern whites who were making a stand for segregation in the schools of Topeka, Kansas.

> There was no way the nature of his mission could be concealed: their efforts up to now simply looked silly.

Gary Powers (right) is arraigned before a Soviet Court – a moment of excruciating embarrassment for Eisenhower's administration, which had gone to elaborate lengths to deny that any U2 spy-flights had taken place.

Little Rock's High School became the improbable scene of a military stand-off in 1957, when the Arkansas authorities tried to enforce continued segregation between black and white students in the city.

The tone is as sweetly reasonable as the content is utterly toxic: this was what passed for 'moderate' white opinion in 1954. On the one hand; on the other; you can see their point; there has to be a middle way ... It's easy to see why Eisenhower isn't revered as a hero of the Civil Rights struggle. And yet, his Presidency saw important advances for African-Americans, however disengaged from their fight he seems to have been.

A good soldier, Eisenhower was a firm believer in the importance of a clear command structure and the importance of obedience and discipline within it. So he was shocked when, in the autumn of 1957, nine black students were excluded from Little Rock High School, in defiance of a ruling by the Supreme Court.

> It's clear from Eisenhower's reaction to the Topeka, Kansas, case that the President's sympathy with the excluded students was very likely limited, but the law was the law, he felt.

It's clear from Eisenhower's reaction to the Topeka, Kansas, case that the President's sympathy with the excluded students was very likely limited, but the law was the law, he felt. He was particularly outraged at the cynical behaviour of State Governor Orval Faubus. His response to threats by white protestors to prevent the 'Little Rock Nine' from being admitted to the school had been to deploy the Arkansas National Guard. Not, however, to stop the white supremacists, but the African-American students – it was the threat of their admission, he said, that had breached the peace.

Eisenhower tried to defuse the situation, summoning the Governor to a meeting. But when the Governor proved obdurate, the President got tough. He first federalized the Arkansas National Guard – its 10,000 members would from now on take their orders

A peaceful, pastoral scene, it seems, but storms of controversy blew up around Eisenhower's Gettysburg farm – much of the equipment (and even land and buildings) had been donated by sometimes shady friends.

from him – and then dispatched the Army's 101st Airborne Division to Little Rock to see the students safely into school.

He'd won the battle, but not of course a war, which still goes on. The 'Little Rock Nine' still faced a long and unpleasant fight. Eisenhower was confirmed in his determination to fight the Southern obstructionists, because if the oppression of black Americans couldn't move him, the indignities suffered by the Constitution could. He was affronted by the fact that African-Americans had a legal right which they were in practice prevented from exercising. He passed his Civil Rights Act of 1957 in the face of the longest

filibuster ever – South Carolina Democrat Strom Thurmond spoke in the Senate for 24 hours and 18 minutes. Amended beyond recognition in the course of debate and then half-heartedly implemented by the authorities in the South, this act unfortunately proved ineffectual. Eisenhower would not rest, but introduced a beefed-up Civil Rights Ac,t which finally became law in May 1960.

Farms and Things

'To the pure, all things are pure,' they say, and that's how it was with Eisenhower, a genuinely high-minded man, who scorned the idea that he might be bought. It seems to have come as a complete surprise to him when critics expressed their concern that he should have accepted lavish gifts from business interests. Eisenhower loved the farm he'd bought himself at Gettysburg, Pennsylvania (right next door to the famous battlefield) and its development and improvement was something of a hobby. So self-evident was it apparently to the President that others would share his enthusiasm that he never questioned the motives of those who helped him make improvements. Livestock, landscaping services, tractors and other equipment, the building of barns and the refurbishment of older buildings; even plots of land, which allowed him to extend his estate. The friends included oilmen W. Alton Jones, B.B. Byers and George E. Allen and associates of Nelson Rockefeller.

More cynical observers looked askance, especially given the concessions the oil industry seemed to have received from the US government during Eisenhower's time in office. Also odd, in light of the fuss that had been made over Truman's appointment of Edwin W.

Pauley as Undersecretary of the Navy, was Eisenhower's appointment of oilman Robert Anderson first as Navy Secretary, then as Defense Secretary and finally as Secretary of the Treasury. He advanced the interests of his own industry in all these roles.

The evidence is there – and pretty damaging it looks, it has to be said. Are we really to believe that the world's most powerful leader can be 'unworldly'? Yet, important as he was, Eisenhower had a childlike air of innocence about him which makes it hard – even now – to believe he could have been corrupt.

Nelson Rockefeller shares a joke with President Eisenhower. The arch-oilman had 'Ike' twisted round his little finger, some said – and his administration did indeed make important concession to big oil.

COLD WAR: COVERT OPERATORS

America entered the 1960s as the undisputed leader of the Free World: pre-eminent politically, economically, and militarily. Yet a certain irritability abroad and an atmosphere of suspicion and skulduggery at home suggested a superpower that wasn't quite comfortable in its own skin.

---◆---

'Efforts and courage are not enough without purpose and direction.'

Eisenhower's authority was immense, but it was in a certain sense historical: he derived his status from his commanding role in World War II. The United States had never really stood down after that conflict: the 'Race to the Rhine' between the Red Army and the Western Allies had got the post-war era off to a jumpy and ill-tempered start; the confrontation between the superpowers was going to shape the world over four decades. In these circumstances, it made sense to have a soldier in the White House, but

John F. Kennedy (left) all optimism and youthful vigour and Richard Nixon (above) all crabby cynicism presented the Presidency in very different lights. But beneath the surface, the similarities were greater than they seemed.

Eisenhower had been in his sixties when he came to office, and if he wasn't yesterday's man, he wasn't tomorrow's either. Chilly as the Cold War climate was, America was a winner, the leading force in the Free World; business was booming and industry was thriving. Wasn't it time this buoyancy and vigour were reflected in the Presidency? Americans were in a mood to look forward now.

JOHN F. KENNEDY, 1961–3

The Kennedy clan would clearly warrant a 'dark history' all to itself. Its members are often regarded as 'American Royalty': an apt enough label – but aptly paradoxical too for a family who've played a profoundly ambiguous part in the modern American story. Today we're all at home with ideas like 'image', 'media management', 'celebrity culture', 'style icons' and so forth – we see through these things, even if we

ANTI-SEMITIC SYMPATHIES

'KIKES', HE CALLED THEM, or 'Sheenies': Joseph Kennedy didn't much like the Jews. 'As a race they stink,' he said. 'They spoil everything they touch.' Such views weren't as unusual in the America of the 1930s as we might like to think. Yet Kennedy carried it to extremes. An intensely egotistical, arrogant man, he was impatient with the give and take of democratic government and made no secret of his sympathy with Hitler's aims. As late as the autumn of 1940, he was making unauthorized approaches to Adolf Hitler, in hopes of attaining 'a better understanding' between Germany and the United States. That November, his public avowal of the view that democracy was 'finished' finished him as a diplomat – and future presidential prospect. He'd have to invest his hopes and ambitions in his sons instead.

somehow can't resist their power. The 'Kennedy Mystique' was arguably the first of these confections, and it embodies the paradox to perfection: its tragedies have been as real as the glamour that's given them their grandeur has been false.

This most elegant of political dynasties had a truly loathsome progenitor. Joseph P. Kennedy was a cold and calculating man. Having made a fortune on the stock market, he involved himself in real estate and in the import–export business. Nothing if not shrewd, he'd built a formidable network of contacts in Boston's Catholic Democratic machine – and, it was widely believed, with bootleggers and gangsters he'd come to know in the Prohibition era. He'd also invested heavily in the movie industry, eventually founding RKO in 1928 and becoming a major mover and shaker in the business. Whilst he clearly enjoyed the access this gave him to available actresses – and to serious stars like Gloria Swanson, with whom notoriously he had an affair – no one could have been less susceptible to the romance of Hollywood. What he seems to have sensed, even at this early stage, was the extent to which not just the print and broadcast news but the wider media were coming to influence opinion and the public mood.

His influence extended into government: cosying up to Franklin D. Roosevelt, by 1938 he'd managed to swing himself the post of American Ambassador to

A schemer, a Nazi sympathizer and a coward, Joseph Kennedy was viewed with fear and loathing by many people in his own generation. Yet the dynasty he founded was to be generally revered.

Great Britain. It was a triumph too far: Kennedy quickly came unstuck in an England on the brink of war with utterances which went from the simply insensitive to the downright fascistic. When the shooting started and the 'Blitz' began, 'Jittery Joe' earned the contempt of his hosts for the panic-stricken

> What he seems to have sensed, even at this early stage, was the extent to which not just the print and broadcast news but the wider media were coming to influence opinion and the public mood.

way he scuttled out of the capital to stay in the countryside each night, well away from the wave of air raids which had just begun.

Kennedy & Sons

It was becoming clear that Joseph wasn't going to make it to the White House, so instead he settled for grooming Joe Jr, his eldest son. He was already making a name for himself as a bomber pilot, his quiet courage in stark contrast with his father's cowardice. But his father's political disgrace had left Joe Jr a lot to live down. Was it this that impelled him to ever more reckless acts of bravery? In 1944, he volunteered to take part in Operation Aphrodite. Quite simply, the plan was to pack aircraft completely full with high-explosive and then direct them at their targets like

Not just a war hero and an accomplished speaker but the most dashing, personally attractive young politician anyone had seen for quite some long time, 'J.F.K.' quickly won the heart of the American electorate.

missiles. Once they were airborne, these flying bombs could be controlled remotely by the crews of shadowing aircraft, but someone had to get them into the air. This could all too easily turn out a suicide mission. So it certainly turned out for Joe Jr. The B-24 Liberator he was piloting blew up prematurely – before it had even made it across the English coast.

The focus shifted on to Jack. We have no reason to think he questioned his second-choice status. Both boys had been brought up in the assumption that the

prestige of the family (and thereby their father) would come first. Jack doesn't seem to have been to blame – as later critics charged – when the torpedo boat he was commanding in the Pacific was run down by a Japanese destroyer, but he himself felt uneasy about the heroic status he was accorded. In an operation which had been mismanaged overall, *PT-109* had been in the wrong place at the wrong time – as far as it went, though, Lieutenant Kennedy had shown commendable courage and presence-of-mind. Thanks in large part to him, he and his crew survived and evaded capture. But his bravery was debased when his father pulled some cinematic strings and Jack's exploits on *PT-109*, exaggerated and distorted, were made the subject of an opportunistic movie.

Not that anyone saw it that way just then. Instead, the young hero was fêted; the all but automatic choice for the Democrats in 1960. His Catholicism may have counted against him in the fight for the nomination, but his war record spoke for itself, while he too spoke with thrilling eloquence of a 'New Frontier'. Success was sealed when he wiped the floor with Republican rival Richard Nixon in the first ever televised Presidential Debate – not so much by what he said, but with his youthful good looks and his easy manner. Nixon was by any standards a formidable opponent ('Tricky Dicky' was, of course, still to write his own chapter in the dark history of the Presidency). On TV, though, he seemed old, crabby and uncomfortable beside his challenger: Kennedy was creating a new way of 'being Presidential'.

It was good old-fashioned machine politics that paved his road to the White House, however. There were widespread claims of fraud in Texas (Vice President Johnson's state) and in Illinois, where Mayor Daly (and allegedly the Mafia) got to work. Claims that the dead got up and walked – and voted – there,

A LIFE DESTROYED

JACK'S LITTLE SISTER, Joseph's eldest daughter Rosemary suffered violent mood-swings from adolescence on; she was subjected to a prefrontal lobotomy in 1941 at the age of 23. This 'calmed' her so completely as to turn her into a childlike imbecile. With hindsight, it seems natural to ask why the family had felt impelled to take this action – to prevent her revealing her sexual abuse by her father, it's been suggested. Whether this was true we've no way of knowing: it's equally possible that the family felt it had to act to protect its political 'honour'; in her more manic moods Rosemary

was slipping out of her school dormitory at night and getting up to who knew what. Either way, it seems astonishingly high-handed now, though it has to be recalled that – though relatively untried – the operation she endured was believed to be quite feasible. It wasn't necessarily 'meant' for her to end up that way.

Outwardly elegant and poised, Rose's possibilities were severely restricted by her mental health. Her story was certainly sad: it may even have been sinister, the darkest secret of the Kennedy clan.

marshalled Frank Costello, mobster and long-time friend of Joseph Kennedy, Frank Costello, have been persistent, but were never proven.

Camelot, Shamalot

With its dashing young President and his beautiful First Lady, the Kennedy White House had an almost palpable aura of idealism and hope. Hence its identification with Camelot, the legendary court of King Arthur, in medieval England, with its gallant knights and ladies fair, just recently brought to the Broadway stage in the famous musical of that name. This was all a bit of a fairytale. The reality was a President who was barely up to the job and out-of-control in his personal life, and a First Lady adrift in her own world of self-absorption.

Despite the image of youthful vigour, John F. Kennedy was in poor health. From adolescence on, he'd had to take antihistamines for a range of allergies as well as drugs for disorders of the upper bowel and

Over time the pharmaceutical cocktail he'd been taking caused severe bone-degeneration, leading some of the vertebrae in his spine to collapse. He had to take more-and-more painkillers just to carry on.

urinary tract. At the age of 30, Addison's disease was added to his list of ills. This affected his adrenal gland, which managed his body's blood sugar and its response to stress. The steroids he took for this complaint caused unpredictable mood-swings. As historian Robert Dallek reported in 2002, after at last being granted access to the late President's medical records, Kennedy had been secretly hospitalized no fewer than nine times during the 1950s. Over time, the pharmaceutical cocktail he'd been taking caused severe bone-degeneration, leading some of the vertebrae in

John F. Kennedy and Jacqueline Bouvier made the perfect couple, male and female paragons of America as it now saw itself. Her grace and sophistication complemented his good looks, strength and energy.

his spine to collapse. He had to take more and more pain-killers just to carry on.

The drugs may also have had the side-effect of increasing his sexual appetites – though the Kennedy brothers, like many young men brought up for power and entitlement, appear to have taken it for granted that women were there to service them. And there's no doubt that many women were seduced by that

certainty and self-assurance – and subsequently, of course, by Kennedy's power as President. But JFK's philandering was well-nigh pathological in its relentlessness and urgency. His conquests are generally numbered in the hundreds, though of course no one really knows. He was driven, compulsive in his desires; unceremonious in his style. Camelot's King Arthur was no romantic, that's for sure. There don't appear to

FOREVER JACKIE

JACKIE KENNEDY, BORN JACQUELINE BOUVIER, wasn't quite as French as her surname makes her sound, though there's no doubt she lent a certain sophistication and style to her husband's household. Her own father had been rampant in his womanizing, which may have helped her take her husband's indefatigable straying in her stride. Protective of her own privacy, she still lent grace to public occasions and she showed real flair and fashionable taste in her restoration of the White House. The death of their second son, Patrick Bouvier Kennedy, in 1963, at the age of just two days, seems to have upset both parents greatly, whilst seeing her husband slain beside her that same year was obviously a lasting trauma. Not surprisingly, perhaps, she preferred to remember the more agreeable aspects of her marriage: she did much to create the cult of 'Camelot', indeed. One result was that, when she eventually tried to move on, marrying the Greek shipping tycoon Aristotle Onassis in 1968, there was some public disappointment in 'Jackie O'. But this was nothing to the

outrage caused by claims by biographer David Heymann in 2009 that – shortly after Jack's assassination – she'd had an affair with her own brother-in-law Robert Kennedy and, the following year, a fling with the actor Marlon Brando.

When he quipped that politics was 'showbiz for ugly people', Jay Leno was forgetting about J.F.K. and Jackie. She lent a whole new glamour to the position of first lady. She became a style icon of her time.

have been any chocolates or flowers – or even foreplay – from this particular chevalier. It seems to have been more Wham, Bam and (if you were very lucky) Thank You Ma'am. Jackie herself complained to a friend that the fabled lover wasn't up to scratch in the sack: 'He just goes too fast and falls asleep,' she said.

Norma Jean, Jack and Bob

Most of John F. Kennedy's sexual encounters were quick-fire one-offs, though there do seem to have been some longer-term affairs, most notoriously with Marilyn Monroe. Notoriously, not just because she was already iconic, the ultimate in sexy femininity, but because of the other company she was known to keep. No starlet got too far in Hollywood in those days without making her accommodation with the Mob.

Marilyn too was underwhelmed by the sexual prowess of the President, if author Robert Slatzer is to be believed. 'He made love like an adolescent,' she'd apparently complained. Despite this, her biographer Anthony Summers said that the screen goddess had been head-over-heels in love with Jack; so much so that she became something of a stalker. In the end, embarrassed by her ceaseless phone calls, the President had brushed her off comprehensively, at which point she'd taken up with his brother Bobby. Despite his lack of legal training, Robert Kennedy had been appointed Attorney General. As such he'd made no secret of his resolve to crack down on organized crime.

This would have been viewed as a provocation by men like Teamsters' boss Jimmy Hoffa and Chicago Mafia chief Sam Giancana, even without the widespread perception that the Kennedys 'owed' them

big. One conspiracy theory has it that they were so angered by Robert's actions that they murdered Marilyn, faking her suicide to smear her lover.

Cuban Crises

Kennedy, it's claimed, wasn't any more accomplished as a leader than as a lover. He badly mishandled the Bay of Pigs invasion of April 1961. Emigré Cuban fighters desperate to dislodge the Communist leader Fidel Castro from their country had received support and training from the CIA under Eisenhower. Kennedy approved the invasion but, anxious to ensure 'deniability', withdrew vital air-support at the eleventh hour. The invasion was an ignominious failure, while the flamboyant 'Fidel' saw his status as left-wing poster-boy assured: revolutionary movements around the world drew encouragement from America's embarrassment.

Kennedy had a better time of it the following year, when the Soviet leader Nikita Khrushchev installed missiles in Cuba, threatening America. The consensus has been that in the stand-off that followed, while 'the world held its breath', President Kennedy held firm while 'Khrushchev blinked'. Only two decades later did it emerge that while the premiers' poker-game continued, an ill-tempered encounter between the American destroyer USS *Beale* and a Soviet submarine had very nearly precipitated a nuclear shooting war.

Some insist that Cuba was Kennedy's nemesis in any case – not because of its Cold War allegiances but its old associations with the Mob. Whatever the other rights and wrongs of Castro's revolution, it had deprived organized crime of the extremely lucrative casino resorts they had run on the island, under the protection of the previous Batista regime. Conspiracy theorists suggest that the Mafia had brought John F. Kennedy to power on the understanding that he'd make it a priority to get them their cash-cow back. His failure to do so sealed his fate.

Left: It seems almost inevitable in hindsight that two of the most iconic figures of their era should have been connected, but some have suggested that Marilyn Monroe was seriously in love with the President.

One Day in Dallas

For it was the Mafia, such theorists say, who had the President shot dead in Dallas on 22 November 1963. And it's easy to see why conspiracy theories abounded. The shock that so young and popular a President should have been gunned down, along with the confusion that followed, made speculation of this sort inevitable. It certainly seemed suspicious that the apparent assassin, Lee Harvey Oswald, was shot dead before he could appear in court. And by Jack Ruby, a night-club-owner who (some suggested) had links with

Below: Bearded and beret-ed, right, Cuban leader Fidel Castro looks cheerful in the aftermath of the Bay of Pigs attack. As well he might: the American-backed invaders had been ignominiously sent packing.

Smiles of admiration and affection for the President and First Lady as they set off on their drive through downtown Dallas on 22 November 1963: who could have guessed at the horrors so soon to come?

the Mob. An entire field of assassination-ology has opened up in the years since, all magic bullets and grassy knolls, leaving things still more confused than they were at the start. Inconsistent witness-testimony, lost records and other unaccountable gaps in the evidence led to widespread scepticism about the findings of the Warren Commission, set up to sift all the data in the assassination's aftermath.

The problem is that the 'facts' are fluid enough to support all sorts of different explanations. Oliver Stone's movie *JFK* (1991), for instance, sees its subject as a liberal idealist, cruelly cut down by agents of the military-industrial complex, concerned that he was going to rob them of their war in Vietnam. The reality is that Kennedy had greatly increased America's commitment to South Vietnam, whilst agreeing to the overthrow of the dictator Diem, creating a power vacuum and making war in that country more or less a matter of time.

LYNDON B. JOHNSON, 1963–9

But it was under Kennedy's successor that the Vietnam War began in earnest. If ever there was an American Tragedy, this was it, with some 60,000 American servicemen killed. Not that it was exactly comic for the Vietnamese, of course: over five million of them were killed and large areas of their country (and surrounding states) laid waste. Also substantially destroyed was the respect for America's democratic institutions.

In 1964 the war started out, as it would continue, with lies: an 'attack' on US warships that hadn't really happened. Lyndon Johnson admitted that himself just four years later, in 1968. Without the Gulf of Tonkin Incident and the outrage it allowed the administration to whip up in the Western press, however, there wouldn't have been a pretext for escalation. Americans were complacent, trusting in their enormous advantage in technology and wealth: 'They can't even make ice cubes,' JFK's Defense Secretary Robert McNamara had sneered. But they could fight with resource and resilience – and they could take casualties in a way that America couldn't. Gradually, they would wear America down.

Most Vietnamese saw no alternative to resisting the occupiers, however hard and painful the fight, while many Americans didn't see the struggle as essential. Society was becoming increasingly paralyzed. Distrust of the government among the sons and daughters of the white middle class dovetailed with mounting anger among African-Americans still marching for their civil rights – and disproportionately affected by the Draft. In this regard, Lyndon Johnson's Presidency wasn't quite the disaster many thought it to be. Under Eisenhower, he'd steered the Civil Rights Act of 1957 through the Senate, and now he did more for African-Americans than Kennedy had ever contemplated doing. But

Lyndon Johnson – perhaps not entirely justly – bore the full brunt of public outrage at the morality of the Vietnam War and of growing weariness at the toll it was taking on the lives of young Americans.

Lyndon Johnson was no J.F.K. Indeed, he sneeringly set himself up as a sort of anti-Kennedy: crude and gross in his self-presentation, he was brusque and brutal in his style of government.

expectations were that much greater; and feelings running much higher, whilst the Vietnam War was a running sore. Johnson's over-optimistic testimony to successive House committees and his secret escalation of the conflict had long since brought America past the point of turning back.

Lyndon Johnson made a good hate-figure: a bully, a boor and a thug, he hectored opponents and hassled friends into doing what he wanted. Was his grossness deliberately designed to humiliate? As a Senator he'd urinate in his office sink while conducting meetings; as President he'd talk to underlings while sitting on the toilet. Foul-mouthed and scatological, he turned his White House into a sort of anti-Camelot, coarse and vulgar. He was damned if he was going to look like he was trying to emulate his predecessor's patrician poise.

WINNING WAYS

JOHNSON'S COURTSHIP OF CLAUDIA ALTA ('Lady Bird') in 1934 was typically brutal. He basically bullied her until he got his way. Her father hadn't approved of him; she herself had wanted to wait, but he'd bombarded her with letters, pressing her to commit to him. He finally drove all the way down to Texas, from Washington, where he was working as a Congressman's secretary, and told her it was now or never. She gave in, as from that time she did to pretty much everything. She accepted his womanizing, albeit unhappily, as his right. As a rising politician, Johnson saw sex as a prize of power. As President, he clearly felt he was in some sort of competition with his predecessor, once boasting that he'd 'had more women by accident than Kennedy had on purpose'. One mistress, Madeleine Brown, stands out: in a newspaper interview after Johnson's death, this Texan woman claimed to have conducted an affair with him over two decades and to have borne him a son. She also hinted that he'd had advance knowledge of the Kennedy assassination.

The long-suffering 'Lady Bird' had to put up with just as many infidelities on her husband's part as her predecessor had, though no one would have dreamt of describing Lyndon Johnson as attractive.

RICHARD NIXON, 1969–74

Richard Nixon (eventually) did his best to disengage from Vietnam, enforced desegregation in the South, and thawed out the Cold War a little with his engagement – *détente* – with China. It's as well to bear those things in mind as we recall his most notorious distinction – that of being the only US President ever to have been forced to resign from office. Many another *should* have been, perhaps, yet, tempting as it is to imagine that his main crime was getting caught, there's no doubt that the charge sheet against Nixon was long and colourful.

In the infamous White House Tapes, over 2000 hours of 'expletive-deleted' bombast and bile, the picture emerged of a foul-mouthed, coarse-minded slob. But bad language was hardly the 37th President's greatest sin. 'You're so goddamned concerned about civilians,' he sneered at (of all people) Henry Kissinger, the Secretary of State with whom he'd planned the secret bombing of neutral Cambodia in 1969–70. This campaign is thought to have claimed over half a million

---

Congress was by-passed on everything that mattered. Typically, they gathered, not in the Oval Office nor even the White House but an adjacent building on Pennsylvania Avenue, in the anonymity of 'Room 175.'

---

civilian lives, but nobody was ever brought to book. Later, in 1973, Nixon is believed to have told the CIA to back a coup against Chile's elected left-wing President, Salvador Allende, having first ordered disruption in that country to 'make the economy scream'. Thousands were murdered and many more interned and tortured when the military dictator Augusto Pinochet seized power. He had a very strong feeling of bitterness and rage against perceived enemies within and actual enemies abroad.

And yet, he was always calculating; always (just about) in control. 'Tricky Dicky' had won his nickname in 1950 when he'd lied and smeared his way on to the Senate, after a vicious campaign against

Helen Gahagan Douglas, whom he'd accused of being a secret Communist. In no time, he'd been in trouble himself, having received an $18,000 ($105,000 today) slush fund from friendly businessmen. With no defence against this charge, he defended himself instead against a criticism no one had made: of keeping Checkers, a spaniel his young daughter had been given by a supporter. An ever-sentimental electorate were happy to be led astray by his plea to be allowed to keep his little girl's pet. Nixon lived to lie and cheat another day.

The Hong Kong Connection

Marianna Liu was working as a cocktail waitress at the Hong Kong Hilton when she met Richard Nixon in 1966, she said. She'd later had a drink with the then-Vice President and his banker-friend Charles 'Bebe' Rebozo in Nixon's room. J. Edgar Hoover had that room watched, and hinted at an intimate relationship, though both parties denied this strenuously. Hoover had a dirty mind and took a puerile pleasure in discomfiting others, so it's quite possible he was mischief-making. But there *were* reports that the FBI Chief feared the waitress might be working as a spy for the Communists. Marianna's father had been an officer in the People's Liberation Army, though she herself had come to British-administered Hong Kong to live with an uncle as a small child.

Three years after that meeting with Nixon, she came to live in the United States. The job-offer that enabled her to immigrate was as housekeeper to a couple in Whittier, California, on Nixon's home patch. No more than a coincidence, she insisted; and Nixon angrily rejected reports that they'd continued to see each other while he was in the White House.

Co-Conspirators

In truth, the White House Tapes bear testimony to the new and rather sinister style of government Nixon developed with the likes of Kissinger, Chiefs of Staff Bob Haldeman and Alexander Haig, and Assistant for Domestic Affairs John Ehrlichman. Congress was by-passed on everything that mattered. Typically, they gathered, not in the Oval Office nor even in the White House but in an adjacent building on Pennsylvania Avenue, in the anonymity of 'Room 175'. Secrecy was a habit, even a compulsion for Nixon. The idea of going through regular channels seems to have been

unthinkable to him. The tone of his meetings with his staff was more in keeping with a criminal conspiracy than a Cabinet. In a sense, of course, that's because that's what it was.

Certainly, that was how it seemed when, one night in June 1972, a group of five burglars was apprehended at Washington's Watergate office complex. They had been trying to break into the

A dangerous double-act, the Nixon and Kissinger days are widely discussed, from the controversial incidents in Southeast Asia to their 'shuttle diplomacy' with China that made the world a little more secure.

headquarters of the Democratic National Committee, and were equipped not just with burglars' tools but listening devices. Three were Cubans, veterans of the Bay of Pigs; one had helped train Cuban émigrés for the CIA; the fifth was a member of CREEP (the Campaign to Re-elect the President). Despite evidence of payments received from CREEP, the Republicans managed to brazen the business out – and even make indignant accusations of Democrat dirty tricks.

But Bob Woodward and Carl Bernstein of the *Washington Post* pressed harder and more persistently and eventually uncovered evidence of a gang of 'plumbers' – in witty reference to their primary role of

AGNEW'S AGONY

IT'S EASILY FORGOTTEN, given Nixon's nightmare descent into the moral mire, that 'Tricky Dicky' and his Watergate co-conspirators were not the only criminals. His administration didn't just lose its President but scored a dismal double-whammy by managing to lose a Vice President as well. Spiro Agnew didn't even manage to make it as far as the Watergate scandal. By the time that broke, he'd been forced from office, a pattern of corruption having been uncovered dating back to his time as a Maryland state official – and eventually Governor – in the 1960s. He'd taken bribes from contractors seeking work for the government. He doesn't seem to have had any involvement in Watergate or the other political crimes associated with it: he was outside that loop, and had other fish to fry. He managed to avoid prosecution (and the jail sentence which would surely have followed) by confessing to the lesser charge of tax evasion and resigning for the sake of the 'national interest'. Nixon wrote to him, praising his patriotic self-sacrifice: the Vice President had shown 'courage and candor', he said. By the President's own standards, of course, he had.

In 1973, Spiro Agnew became the only US Vice President to have to resign over criminal charges – though his transgressions were to seem trivial when those of his political master emerged.

stopping leaks. They'd evidently gone much farther, though. At the behest of Presidential aides like E. Howard Hunt and Gordon Liddy, they'd been illegally wiretapping human rights, women's liberation and anti-war activists and using forged documents to smear famous Democrats – including the late President John F. Kennedy. They'd relied on Cuban émigrés, confirmed in their right-wing sympathies and skilled in clandestine work after years of fighting against Castro.

With the dirty linen coming thick and fast, a Senate committee was called to investigate. Nixon had no

> Nixon is said to have ordered wiretraps on his brother Donald's phone – though at times one wonders whether there was anybody's phone the President of Paranoia didn't wiretap.

The Senate Watergate Committee had to sit for over more than a year, from May 1973. Nixon and his co-conspirator made them fight for every file, every memo, every tape, every word of testimony.

alternative but to promise cooperation. Haldeman, Ehrlichman and Attorney General Richard Kleindienst were all forced to resign. White House Counsel John Dean made his own deal with the Senate investigators: his testimony tied Nixon into the conspiracy. Even then, the 'smoking gun' which would convict him proved elusive until, after months of frantic resistance, he was finally compelled to hand over the White House Tapes. Lengthy sections had been wiped – without any explanation being forthcoming. Crucially, though, still recorded loud and clear was a conversation in which he tried to get the FBI to stop the investigation into the Watergate burglaries. Even then, he clung on to office: finally, on 8 August 1974, with proceedings already in hand to remove him by impeachment, he announced that he would 'put the interests of America first'. Even then, no admission of guilt was made.

A BEEF WITH BROTHER

WHAT IS IT WITH PRESIDENTIAL BROTHERS? Nixon is said to have ordered wiretaps on his brother Donald's phone – though at times one wonders whether there was anybody's phone the President of Paranoia *didn't* wiretap. Yet little brother certainly needed careful watching. In the 1950s, as Richard was starting to make a name for himself on the Senate, Donald decided to cash in on that name by opening up his own chain of restaurants, selling 'Nixonburgers'. So far, so tacky: it was all a bit embarrassing for Richard, but no worse. By 1956, though, he was a rising star as Vice President to Eisenhower, while Nixon's Restaurants were sinking fast. With Donald looking frantically round for white knights, the not-so-spotless figure of Howard Hughes came riding to the rescue with a bail-out of $205,000 ($1.6 million today). No one seriously believed that the wealthy recluse was helping hapless Donald out of the kindness of his heart: Richard Nixon had to protest his innocence. The issue dogged him through his electoral fight with Kennedy and the 'Nixonburger' gibes followed him into the Presidency – though by that time he'd have bigger problems to face.

Nixon did his best to depart with dignity, presenting his resignation as an act of patriotic self-sacrifice. Voters weren't fooled, though the political establishment were eager to forgive and forget.

GERALD FORD, 1974–7

Almost as shocking as Nixon's conduct in office was his subsequent rehabilitation. Five Presidents were to attend his funeral in 1994. Heavy-hitting journalists lined up to praise his vision, his insight, his experience; his contribution to American life, 'whatever his faults'. It's good to be big-hearted, of course; and generous to forgive – though it helps if the sinner shows some regret for (or even real consciousness of) what he's done. And it's hard not to suspect a less worthy, more opportunistic motive behind this magnanimity: America's political elite was setting the bar very low for itself for the years to come.

Even so, it had the decency to be shocked when, within a month of 'Tricky Dicky's' departure from office, he was pardoned by his Vice President and successor, Gerald Ford. One of the more decent men to occupy the Presidency, Ford was also among the more inept: his action called his own credibility into question right away. As far as the media and public were concerned, it looked like one more crooked deal on the ex-President's part; one more cynical abuse of Presidential power. It didn't help that Ford allowed himself to be pushed around by former Nixon aides like Alexander Haig (who'd postured as America's 'acting President' during the interregnum). Nixon, as we've seen, had conducted most of the business of government in secret, specifically excluding his official hierarchy – his former deputy didn't have a clue.

Johnson's gibe that Ford couldn't 'fart and chew gum at the same time' (anxiously amended to 'walk and chew gum' in later press reports) was about as fair as most of Johnson's pronouncements on his rivals and colleagues. In truth, the college athlete and football-jock was highly intelligent – though also, in some ways a simple soul. By instincts a peacemaker, a smoother-over of quarrels, he was also under immense personal

Gerald Ford's promptness in pardoning Nixon reflected well on his personal compassion but less so on his political instincts. Far from drawing a line under Watergate, it caused the scandal to rumble on.

Gerald Ford asked Vice President Nelson Rockefeller to undertake an investigation into allegations of illegal domestic activities by the CIA in 1975, following up the findings of the Church Commission the year before.

strain on taking office since his beloved wife Betty had breast cancer and was about to have a mastectomy. He could see that America was hurting; by pardoning the rogue President, he hoped he'd be waving a wand to make the pain and bitterness go away. *He* would have been prostrate with shame and guilt if he'd been caught out in the merest fraction of what Nixon had done, and he took pity on what he fondly imagined was Nixon's suffering.

Company Crimes

Straightforward as he was, he was constantly undercut by the actions and briefings of his staff, including Henry Kissinger and Donald Rumsfeld. Despite the President's support for the 1974 Church Commission in probing CIA 'dirty tricks' (including assassinations) and his establishment of the Rockefeller Commission in 1975 to take things farther, it is said that they did their best to limit the investigations' scope. Even so, John Church and his fellow-Senators especially uncovered a catalogue of crimes, most notoriously

the assassination plots against Fidel Castro. It wasn't just the illegality but the farcical nature of these (exploding cigars, depilatories to make the macho Cuban leader lose his beard ...): America was exposed to ridicule. Earlier targets had included Rafael Trujillo, dictator of the Dominican Republic, and the Congolese leader Patrice Lumumba in the 1950s. It also came to light that, as part of Project MK-Ultra from the 1950s to the 1970s, experiments had been conducted in the use of LSD as a possible aid to interrogation: soldiers and mental patients were used without their informed (or indeed any) consent.

First Watergate; now this; America's international reputation was in tatters. But – at least for the moment – Americans felt more relief than humiliation when, at the end of April 1975, the Fall of Saigon brought US

BETTY'S LITTLE HELPERS

BORN ELIZABETH ANNE BLOOMER, Ford's First Lady had been a model and then a dancer before she met and married the future-President of the United States. But that resumé wasn't quite as risqué as her husband's opponents liked to imply: she'd founded her own company to take dance to disabled children. As First Lady, 'Betty' wasn't one to smile sweetly and keep her mouth shut: she gave outspoken support for the Equal Rights Amendment (ERA). She was no more shy of expressing her live-and-let-live views on pre-marital sex and even marijuana use. Such views were bound to alienate more conservative Americans, though her outspoken honesty won her great respect.

Betty Ford built a lasting legacy with the work she did in publicizing the problems of addiction – from which she herself had suffered. She gave her name to one of the world's foremost treatment centres.

Betty was initially with less forthcoming about her addictions to alcohol and painkillers (the latter prescribed while she was receiving cancer treatment). But she gave full disclosure in her later memoirs and turned her experiences to the best possible account in 1982 when she founded the Betty Ford Center at Rancho Mirage, California, with the help of her friend, the diplomat and philanthropist Leonard Firestone.

Earl Butz's fateful joke was the sort of thing which had passed as wit in Republican circles for as long as anyone could remember. It was surely a good sign that it seemed so outrageous now.

involvement in Vietnam to a dramatic if undignified end. It was a 'defeat' that brought Ford out slightly ahead.

Inappropriate Appointments

If Ford had inherited several of his scandals, some of his own decisions were to blow up in his face: one of these was his appointment of Nelson Rockefeller as his Vice President. That choice was already controversial – Rockefeller was far too liberal for conservative Republicans – and then it emerged that the oilman had given generous gifts to establishment figures like Henry Kissinger. Nixon supporters (there were still some on the Right) suspected Kissinger of having had a hand in their hero's downfall, along with Alexander Haig, another Rockefeller protégé.

As for Agriculture Secretary Earl Butz, he beggared belief when his views on the race question emerged into the public domain in 1976. He'd been flying back to California after that year's Republican National Convention, chatting with singing star Pat Boone and former White House Counsel John Dean. Asked by Boone why the Grand Old Party couldn't seem to attract more black supporters, Butz had replied:
'The only thing the coloreds are looking for in life are tight pussy, loose shoes and a warm place to shit'.

It was good news of a sort, that Dean and Boone don't seem to have been much impressed. This kind of 'humour' had been the everyday stuff of manly banter in both parties in former times. Challenged on what he'd said when the remark appeared in the press, Butz made early (and typically unscrupulous) use of the 'taken out of context' defence, and Ford for a time appeared inclined to let it go. But amidst clamorous demands by protestors that he come down off the fence

and start to 'Kick Butz', he was forced to accept his Agriculture Secretary's resignation.

Stray Shots

For all his athletic background, Ford could be physically uncoordinated; pictures of his pratfalls on

> If Ford had inherited several of his scandals, some of his own decisions were to blow up in his face: one of these was his appointment of Nelson Rockefeller as his Vice President.

Yet another unfortunate entrance by this the most accident-prone of presidents: Gerald Ford hits Austria the hard way when he is caught on camera taking a tumble down the steps of Air Force 1.

the ski slopes were widely reproduced. Most notoriously, on arriving in Austria on a visit, he tripped and fell down the steps of Air Force 1, an incident famously spoofed by the TV comic Chevy Chase. His golf-shots were wild on occasion: in 1977, a spectator was hit on the head by the Presidential ball at a pro-celebrity tournament at North Hills Country Club, at Menomonee Falls, Wisconsin; ironically, he was to catch a boy-bystander on the leg on the same golf course seven years later.

Fortunately for him, his would-be assassins were equally accident-prone: two attempts made within a few weeks of each other in 1975 were foiled, his clumsy or hesitant attackers being successfully

disarmed, the first by a Secret Serviceman, the second by a brave bystander.

JIMMY CARTER, 1977–81

Ford's clumsiness wasn't just physical: there were verbal stumbles too. It was to general shock and disbelief that, in his 1976 re-election campaign, the President insisted, 'There is no Soviet domination in eastern Europe.' Fortunately for him, he was pitched against an opponent in Jimmy Carter who was almost as hapless as he was himself. Ford's Republican supporters had no illusions: the Nixon Pardon had severely damaged an already improbable Presidential candidate – but if anyone could lose against him, Carter could. The Democratic candidate seemed to have been heaven-sent: he'd come from nowhere (well, Georgia – but he had no track record at a national level); voters found it hard to take him

JORDAN'S JUDGEMENT

IT WASN'T JUST HIS FAMILY that embarrassed President Carter. Chief of Staff Hamilton Jordan liked to cut a little too much of a dash in his social life. As the spin doctors say now, he 'let himself become the story'.

It didn't matter that he denied having leered down the décolletage of the Egyptian ambassador's wife, saying that he'd always wanted to see 'the pyramids'. People enjoyed the anecdote – and the administration's discomfiture – too much. It didn't matter that the White House published a 33-page document to discredit claims that he'd spat his drink (an Amaretto and Cream) down the dress of a woman in Sarsfields' Bar: the Washington watering-hole became a sort of pilgrimage site for the satirically-minded. In 1978, he was accused of having snorted cocaine at Studio 54, and though a public investigation acquitted him of the charge it seemed to stick.

Manhattan's Studio 54 nightclub was the place to be seen in the late-70s – but not, Hamilton Jordan discovered, if you were snorting cocaine and you were White House Chief of Staff.

seriously with his folksy manner and his unworldly air; even his background as a peanut farmer seemed vaguely comic.

And while Americans felt guilty about sneering at someone for his piety, they couldn't help finding his moral earnestness unsettling. In an unprecedented presidential candidate's interview with *Playboy* magazine, he solemnly confessed: 'I've looked on a lot of women with lust. I've committed adultery in my heart many times.' This is nothing more than sound Christian doctrine, as laid down in Matthew 5, 28: 'But I say unto you, that every one that looketh on a woman to lust after her, hath committed adultery already with her in his heart.' For most Americans, though, it seemed so over-scrupulous as to be outlandish.

Family Values

Such exaggerated self-castigation inevitably seemed to some like self-righteousness in a backhanded form,

Swigging beer out of a can and playing up to an image he'd have been far better attempting to live down, Billy Carter appeared to revel in the ridicule and the bad name that he brought both on himself and his brother Jimmy.

> Unkindly (albeit not inaccurately) portrayed by the press as a loser, a redneck and a drunk, he reacted by playing up to that image.

and whilst this was almost certainly unfair, it exposed Carter to criticism and ridicule. Especially when his sister Ruth Stapleton Carter – a celebrated preacher – had a well-publicized friendship with pornographer Larry Flynt, the 'King of Smut'. In 1977 she claimed to have converted him to Christianity. And it was true – at least for a time. *Hustler* magazine briefly took on a new and incongruous evangelical Christian slant, but then Larry lost his faith and normal service was resumed.

Billy Carter was a liability even by the standards of presidential brothers. Unkindly (albeit not inaccurately) portrayed by the press as a loser, a redneck and a drunk, he reacted by playing up to that image, endorsing a new brand of 'Billy Beer'. Once, in 1979, he urinated publicly on the runway at Atlanta Airport.

ATTACK OF THE KILLER RABBIT

WHAT DID JIMMY CARTER HAVE TO DO to get himself some dignity? In 1979 he was fishing in a pond outside Plains, Georgia, when he saw a rabbit swimming directly toward his boat. No cuddly bunny this but a large (and apparently excited) swamp rabbit, a spokesman told the press: 'hissing menacingly, its teeth flashing, its nostrils flared'. Sick? Insane? Frantic with fear as it was pursued by some predator? For whatever reason, it seemed to be determined to get into Carter's boat. The President was forced to lash out at it several times with his paddle to see it off.

In integrity and intellect alike, Jimmy Carter had the makings of one of his country's greatest ever presidents. But his political judgement was badly flawed, and his unworldliness was a liability.

He'd been caught short while awaiting the arrival of a Libyan trade delegation he'd invited to Georgia. He was to lead a number of reciprocal delegations to that country himself. When Jews in Georgia objected to an official visit from a country whose dictator Muammar Gaddafi was open in his support for Palestinian terrorism, he was ready with his response: 'There's a hell of a lot more Arabians than Jews.' Billy was subsequently called before a Senate Committee to explain how he'd come to receive $220,000 ($650,000 today) from the Libyan regime.

Laughing Stock

The press and public were having fun at Carter's expense. The President's moral simplicity made him too tempting a target to resist. His virtues counted against him – he had a way of carrying them to such extremes. What kind of President personally takes charge of the schedule for the White House tennis courts? His judgement was called into question when Budget Director Burt Lance, a banker friend of his from Georgia, was found to have been involved in sloppy banking practices in that state. Nothing terribly serious, but, once again, such was Carter's air of probity that the least infraction seemed to represent some catastrophic fall from grace.

Carter had been fortunate that it had fallen to him to fight Gerald Ford and a Republican Party badly damaged by Watergate. In the end, though, he wasn't lucky enough to stay in power. Quite the opposite, in fact. It wasn't his fault that, in the autumn of 1979, the seething discontent of decades boiled over in Iran, or that crowds of angry students seized the US Embassy in Tehran with everyone inside. Neither was it his fault that the military operation to rescue the hostages was an ignominious failure, compounding what was already an American catastrophe. Three helicopters broke down in a sandstorm; other aircraft were lost in the fighting; eight American servicemen were killed – and not a single hostage freed. The new Islamic regime toyed with Carter. They waited till the Presidential election was past before releasing their captives as a goodwill gesture to his successor.

US officials at the Tehran Embassy are shepherded away by their student captors in 1979. The episode was a disaster for Iran–American relations, but the final straw for the Carter presidency.

THE WORLD STAGE: MEDIA, MISSILES AND MISBEHAVIOUR

The end of the Cold War brought a 'New World Order', in which America was emphatically on top. In the White House, though, the Old Order prevailed. Secrecy and skulduggery prevailed as successive presidents sought to evade the attentions of an ever-more powerful global media.

◆

'Government always finds a need for whatever money it gets.'

Scandal depends on secrecy: individuals who are all respectability in the eyes of the world get up to all sorts of mischief when they can't be seen. But it also depends on publicity: what's hidden has to be revealed. By the 1980s, the age of 24-hour TV news was upon us; the print media competed the only way they could, by becoming more intrusive and explicit. It was hard to imagine anything *not* being revealed. In 1985, the state of the President's colon was discussed in detail – and with graphics – on live TV. Secrecy

An improbable president on the face of it, Ronald Reagan was an elderly ex-actor who proved perfectly equipped for an image-conscious age – perhaps more so in some ways than George W. Bush (above).

seemed to be a forgotten concept. So much so that politicians concluded that they'd have to mend their ways, and stop misbehaving? Not a bit of it! They were human beings – and unusually arrogant ones at that. But when the hot, moist front of secret sleaze met the broad, cold front of media scrutiny, heavy showers of scandal was the result.

RONALD REAGAN, 1981–9

For many in the outside world, Ronald Reagan's election came as something of a shock. The idea of an ex-movie actor in the White House seemed incongruous somehow. And not just any movie actor but the man who, in *Knute Rockne, All American* (1940), had uttered the immortally cheesy line 'Win one for the Gipper!'. In introducing the new President to their bewildered publics, those foreign newspapers that didn't opt for the open-faced college football

hero showed stills from *Bedtime for Bonzo* (1951), in which he posed with a chimpanzee. People had serious problems in taking him seriously: 'Governor Ronald Duck', one British writer had called him, in his Sacramento days. Americans didn't seem to have that problem: even when they didn't support or even like the new President, they couldn't help but be aware of his abilities. (For Reagan himself, meanwhile, it wasn't a problem that even arose – his

Images from his various movies regularly haunted the Reagan presidency: here he co-stars with a chimp (and Diana Lynn) in *Bedtime for Bonzo*, 1951. But he shrugged off the derision with a smile.

ability not to take himself too seriously was one of his great strengths.)

His age was rather more controversial: 69 when he was elected for the first time in 1980. Characteristically, though, he was able to turn even this to his advantage. Challenged on the issue in the second Presidential Debate of 1984, in which he was pitted against Democrat Walter Mondale, he pledged not to exploit his opponent's 'youth and inexperience' for political purposes. In truth, as old as he was, Reagan was the future; a new kind of politician. The first 'post-modern President', it might be said, for a newly media-conscious age in which content and presentation were seen as two sides of the same coin.

LIKE FATHER, LIKE SON?

BORN IN 1958, RON JR FOLLOWED his father into showbusiness – but not in quite the way he may have had in mind. One semester into his course at Yale, he left to become a dancer, finding a place with the highly regarded Joffrey Ballet, of Chicago. Married, since 1980, he's always laughed off the inevitable suggestions that he's gay, though the (arguably more damning) charge of being a liberal has stuck. Outspoken in his views on freedom-of-expression issues, he's also made no secret of his atheism – a position he apparently came to at the age of 12. But he held his peace during his father's Presidency, and has since been concerned to distance him from those who've claimed to have taken on the mantle as his successors: Ronald Reagan wouldn't have had any time for Bush's Neocons or the modern-day Republican Right, Ron Jr. says. Yet his elder half-brother Michael disagrees: adopted in infancy by Ronald Reagan and his first wife Jane Wyman, he grew up with many of his father's right-wing views. He is adamant that the late President would have been with the Tea Party movement all the way.

Ron Jr. did things his own way, defying the disapproval of his parents in everything from his career-choice to his political and religious views, though he did his best to avoid embarrassing his father.

Reagan liked nothing better than to be underestimated by his opponents: those who branded him a buffoon were playing the President's game. Here he tries to share his love of jelly beans by offering one to Bill Clinton.

For centuries, politics had been about big speeches and smoke-filled rooms; fiery rhetoric and horse-trading behind the scenes. These still had their place, but political messages were increasingly being marketed like products, while politicians needed an actor's skills. And not those of the stage actor, belting out emotion for the benefit of those in the top-balcony, but those of the movie-star: easy-going and conversational in style, understated in his charisma. Ronald Reagan wasn't a bad orator but, schooled for decades as an actor and TV host, he had a genius for reaching audiences, putting people at their ease. He was definitely a statesman to take seriously.

No Laughing Matter

Not that Reagan didn't have his comic side: he was not just young at heart, but positively childish in some ways, from his love of jellybeans to his rumbustious sense of humour. 'I've signed legislation that will outlaw Russia,' he mock-solemnly intoned in a voice test for a re-election broadcast in 1984: 'We begin bombing in five minutes.' A joke about mutually assured destruction? In the circumstances, a beleaguered Soviet Union wasn't taking any chances. Its armed forces were placed on high alert.

Reagan wasn't always joking when he made outrageous statements, though. What are we to make of his assertion that, with a film crew in Europe, he'd

THE JANUARY SURPRISE

POLITICIANS HAVE ALWAYS TRIED to make the most out of success and put the best possible face on failure. You wouldn't really expect them to do anything else. Likewise, it's natural for them to want there to be good news to give the electorate when it matters the most, in the month before they go to the polls to cast their votes. But the age of wall-to-wall news has also been the age of wall-to-wall news-management, with widespread fears about just how far politicians might be prepared to go. There's been much controversy since about the possibility that the Carter administration was hoping to spring a nice 'October Surprise' for everyone by doing a deal with Iran's Islamic regime to secure the release of the US hostages from the Embassy in time for the 1980 election. And the widely held suspicion that Republican staffers made the Iranians a better offer: they were eventually released just minutes after Reagan's inauguration in 1981. The theory remains very much unproven, but the circumstantial evidence started to look very strong when the Iran–Contra Scandal flared up a few years later.

Was it just a happy coincidence that the Iranian hostages were returned in time to get Ronald Reagan's presidency off to an upbeat start? It's hard to know, but many commentators have their suspicions.

witnessed the liberation of the Nazi concentration camps? He made this claim several times – recalling his 'experience' with apparent emotion – most notably in conversation with Israeli Prime Minister Yitzhak Shamir. It certainly can't be taken as the truth. There was nothing dishonourable about Reagan's service in World War II: he was too short-sighted to be much use in the military and worked hard with the First Motion Picture Unit making movies designed to help in training the military and keeping up morale. But he never once left the continental United States, throughout the entire conflict.

Reagan's worst enemies never believed that the President would say such a thing in a deliberate attempt to deceive – even if that had been his purpose, how could he have hoped not to be caught out? The only convincing conclusion we can come to is that, at some level, it was such a powerful story that he sincerely believed it; this master of presentation had pulled the wool over his own eyes. Even outright lies, of which this doesn't seem to be one, often involve a degree of self-delusion. The subject of lying never ceases to be topical in the area of politics, of course, and UC Santa Barbara psychologist Bella DePaulo has made a celebrated study. She makes the point that lies can be 'like wishes ... when you wish you were a kind of person that you know you're not'.

But the President's sentimentalizing fantasies weren't always quite so harmless. Supporters were stunned at the statement he made before a visit to

Solemn and sincere, Ronald Reagan walks up to lay a wreath at Germany's Bitburg Military Cemetery in 1985. He seems to have had no idea how contentious his conciliatory speech was going to be.

Ronald Reagan wears the white hat of the cowboy hero: his presidency brought to the White House not only a touch of Hollywood glamour but the simplistic morality of the movies.

Germany's Bitburg Military Cemetery in 1985. Those interred included members of the wartime Waffen SS. Asked to cancel the engagement, he refused: the German soldiers too 'were victims ... just as surely as the victims in the concentration camps'. Reagan's words appear to have been intended in part as a gesture of solidarity toward West German Chancellor Helmut Kohl, who'd gone out on a limb for America over the new range of Pershing missiles. But they stemmed in part as well from that simple-hearted assumption he had that there was no quarrel so serious it couldn't be soothed away with warm words and folksy platitudes. Jewish groups weren't anything like so sure.

Ignorance No Defence?

Others too came to feel that Reagan's absent-mindedness wasn't good for democracy. The President's jokes about his own indolence were charming, to be sure. 'I never drink coffee at lunch,' he said. 'I find it keeps me awake for the afternoon.' Most Americans, fed up with being badgered by politicians, found his easy-going approach refreshing. Far from being outraged by his frankly expressed preference for being on the golf course rather than in the Oval Office, they saw it as evidence of his sanity and chuckled when he quipped: 'They say hard work never hurt anybody, but I figure why take the chance.'

More serious observers were concerned that the man who inveighed against the evils of 'big government' seemed to see such a small role for the

President as well. While he dozed, joked and idled around, however, his aides were hard at work – and they were often up to no good. Reagan's government gave substantive support to South Africa's murderous and unabashedly racist white regime, while he himself bumbled on, oblivious. Asked to justify his administration's stance, he assured reporters that Pretoria had 'eliminated the segregation that we once had in this country'. There were no lengths, it seemed,

> Reagan's government gave substantive support to South Africa's murderous and unabashedly racist white regime, while he himself bumbled on, oblivious.

to which the President wouldn't be prepared to go to cover up for a reliable ally in the Cold War struggle.

Nicaragua was a no-brainer, then. Reagan and his staff gave outspoken support to the right-wing Contras in their fight against that country's (elected) Sandinista government. Unable to take on the official military, opposition insurgents – the Contras – carried out a series of atrocities, burning villages, massacring their inhabitants, abducting people, raping women and torturing prisoners. These were testified to by human-rights groups and Catholic missionaries. US support for this spree of murder and rapine caused world-wide controversy – even before it became clear that Reagan's aides had been channelling money to the insurgents behind the back of Congress. It further emerged that, as a way of keeping this support 'off the books', they had been funding it by selling weapons to Iran. This in turn, the administration's accusers claimed, was a way of discreetly rewarding the Iranians for their cooperation over the Embassy hostages back in 1980: a number of conspiracy-theories meshed beautifully in this Iran–Contra Scandal.

'Freedom': the word had an inspirational ring in Reagan's speeches. For the people of Nicaragua, though, it meant something completely different: it meant murder, rape and pillage at the hands of the Contra rebels.

'MOMMY' DEAREST

NANCY AND RONALD REAGAN were famously devoted as a couple: the President affectionately addressed his wife as 'Mommy'. She was cold and distant as a mother, though, their daughter Patti was later to complain. Like Ron Jr, Patti grew up an outspoken liberal – though she was rather more ready than her brother to attack her parents publicly.

Nancy was staunchly loyal to her husband, though she stayed clear of political controversy except in family-oriented issues – such as drugs. Her 'Just Say No' campaign had the virtue of 'no-nonsense' straightforwardness as far as conservatives were concerned; liberal critics said it was too simplistic. Yet, while for the most part she remained behind the scenes, some suggested that Nancy was a real power behind the Presidency. She certainly did her best to manage her husband's time and – as she saw it – protect him from the rigours of his job, especially after the very-nearly-successful assassination attempt of 1981. Americans were intrigued when it emerged that she regularly consulted an astrologer and made modifications to the President's schedule in response.

For most Americans, the abiding memory of this affair was probably the testimony of National Security Council member Oliver North. A picture of military correctness, the ex-Marine admitted to all manner of illegality, all in his view justified by the anti-Communist cause. But the other unforgettable aspect of the investigation by the Tower Commission was the

> The abiding memory of this affair was probably the testimony of National Security Council member Oliver North. A picture of military correctness, the ex-Marine admitted to all manner of illegality, all in his view justified by the anti-Communist cause.

vagueness of the President's replies, when he was summoned: he had 'no recollection' of authorizing arms shipments, he said. Was he up to it? Was he being deliberately evasive? Was this about dodderiness or deniability? Was Reagan's whole 'hands-off' style a way of evading responsibility for the actions taken in his name? Either way, it didn't look too good.

Reagan was equally inattentive, it seems, where the financial dealings of his henchmen were concerned.

His tough law-and-order message applied only to the poor, it seemed. Moral crusader and Presidential Counselor Ed Meese was only the most senior staff-member said to have benefited when the Wedtech Corporation, a military supplier, paid for special access to the administration. Meese's old friend and personal attorney Robert E. Wallach is believed to have brokered the deal, which resulted in Wedtech's being granted a $32 million contract for supplying equipment that the US Army had thought was not good enough. More than 20 staff had to be dismissed from the Environmental Protection Agency (EPA) over one scandal or another, while officials at the Department of Housing and Development (HUD) were found to have granted construction contracts to favoured companies who'd made contributions to Republican Party funds. Meanwhile, Marilyn Harrell was found to have embezzled $5.6 million from the Department of Housing and Development (HUD). She claimed to have given the money to charity, earning herself the newspaper nickname 'Robin HUD'. In the late 1980s and early 1990s, over 700 financial institutions had to be baled out to a tune of $160 billion thanks to ideologically driven 'deregulation' introduced by President and his merry men.

Pretty in pink, Nancy Reagan had a flamboyant femininity that masked a steely side. Her children complained of her coldness, though she was a loyal and protective partner who very clearly loved her husband.

GEORGE H.W. BUSH, 1989–93

Reagan's Vice President had been born to the political purple, his father a senator, his grandfathers both wealthy bankers. He served with distinction in World War II as a Navy flier, before going on to Yale to study economics. Moving to Houston, where he started off in the oil industry in 1948, he quickly made himself a substantial fortune. He began his political career in Texas in the 1960s, running first (and unsuccessfully) for the Senate and then as a Congressman. He attracted criticism for allegedly exaggerating the extent of his connection with that state: 'the only Texan I know who eats lobster with his chilli,' House Speaker Jim Wright would later joke. As a Congressman, Bush was serious enough about his claims to be Texan to maintain a Houston hotel room which he recorded as his 'official residence' – though

cynics suggested that this might have had more to do with a desire to avoid taxes on the family estate he'd inherited at Kennebunkport, Maine.

The Family Firm

In the 1970s, Bush became US Ambassador first to the United Nations, then to China; in 1975 he was appointed Director of the CIA. There were accusations that his family was profiteering. In 1989, in the aftermath of the massacre in Tiananmen Square, Beijing, his brother Prescott defied an official ban on business with China to make an $18 million deal to build a golfing resort outside Shanghai. Sales of satellite technology to China followed: Prescott is believed to have made $250,000 on the deal. He also visited Japan, apparently canvassing for business, just days before George H.W. arrived in his Presidential

Left: A quiet behind-the-scenes operator, George H.W. Bush had been the perfect foil for the exuberant Reagan. As President, he had to work on what he referred to as the 'Vision Thing'.

Below: He was no Billy Carter perhaps, but Prescott Bush still succeeded in embarrassing his President-brother with his well-publicized business dealings in both China and Japan.

capacity. Neil Bush, the President's son, was implicated in the Silverado Savings & Loans collapse: an investigation found 'numerous breaches' of his fiduciary duty, but stopped short of calling for criminal charges.

Given the Bush family's background in banking and oil, and its continuing connections with those worlds, it was no great surprise in hindsight when they were linked with the Bank of Credit & Commerce International (BCCI). Though founded by a Pakistani businessman, this bank had extensive contacts across the Muslim world, including oil-rich Arab states like Saudi Arabia – and hence, naturally enough, with the American oil industry. But BCCI was no ordinary bank. It was finally forced to close in 1991 by international regulators for myriad infractions. Before that, over a number of years, investigators had reported that the bank appeared

> Reagan had taken him on as his running mate in large part because he represented centrist moderation; now he reinvented himself as a right-winger, pushing buttons on business regulation, abortion and taxation.

actively to be soliciting criminal money for laundering from drug smugglers and offering assistance to terrorist groups. Now, as they examined its dealings in depth, they found themselves uncovering an evil financial empire, its conduct riddled with irregularities, its labyrinthine structures apparently specifically designed to impede oversight. The full complexity has yet to be unravelled, as has the true extent of the Bush family's involvement with an institution which brought them into association – albeit indirect – with such surprising company as the Colombian cocaine cartels and the Islamist terrorist Osama bin Laden.

Street-Fighting Man

The US Presidential campaign is never really the place for anyone of a morally delicate disposition, but Bush's

The appointment of Dan Quayle as George Bush's running mate was met with some dismay but their partnership sealed the 1988 election. It's all smiles here as they attend the West Carrollton fourth annual paper festival parade with their wives.

bid of 1989 was particularly unpleasant. The blue-blood set out to show he could rumble in the gutter, and did so in some style. His opponent, Massachusetts' Governor George Dukakis, proved too gallant for his own good, promptly sacking the staffer who tried to make Vice President Bush's marital fidelity an election issue. Bush was playing hardball, though: Reagan had taken him on as his running mate in large part because he represented centrist moderation; now he reinvented himself as a right-winger, pushing buttons on business regulation, abortion and taxation.

And on race – though never explicitly, of course. Since the success of the Civil Rights Movement, that was no longer allowed. Instead, he allowed his team to put out a TV ad attacking the Governor for being soft on crime: he'd approved the scheme which had paroled one Willie Horton from his Massachusetts prison. Convicted of murder 14 years before, he'd been allowed out on weekend furlough and failed to return. He'd gone on to commit armed robbery and rape. And from his photo, it was clear that he was black.

The ad was screened no fewer than 600 times and seen by an estimated 80 million viewers. The aim was to make Willie Horton Dukakis' running-mate, Bush's campaign manager Lee Atwater boasted. African-American groups were in no doubt what the advert's subliminal meaning was. Bush himself had the grace to feel guilty about it, it was said. Bush's campaign was hampered by his choice of Dan 'No Jack Kennedy' Quayle as Vice-Presidential candidate, but in the end he still won comfortably.

Bush's re-election campaign of 1992 was haunted by his headline pledge of 1988 – 'Read my lips: no new taxes!' – which he'd been compelled to break during the course of his first term. The economy was on the slide, and, with the threat from the Soviet Union gone, the Republicans' advantage as the party of strong defence had disappeared. Ironic as this may have been, given the Reagan–Bush government's role in bringing about this conclusion, it left Bush without a clear political purpose – and the American people without a clear motive for electing him.

MATRIARCH AND MISTRESS

BARBARA BUSH EARLY ON ACCEPTED her role as mother to her sons and allowed herself to be defined by it – especially after her daughter Pauline Robinson Bush (or 'Robin') died of leukaemia in 1953. Barbara's hair went grey with shock – and she refused to dye it, feeling that this would be a betrayal of some kind. From that time on, she threw herself into her matriarch's role even more than before; even in the White House she remained mother first, First Lady second. By that time, it was more-than-murmured, her husband had long since found himself a second 'wife at the office' in his personal assistant Jennifer FitzGerald, who'd moved with him to China and subsequently to the CIA. That she was sexually involved with George H.W. Bush has never been officially confirmed, but Washington gossips were never in any doubt.

Barbara Bush was content to take a background role: even as first lady, she played the part of happy homebody, but she was full of ambition for her husband and her sons.

WILLIAM J. CLINTON, 1993–2001

Hillary Rodham found herself a real catch when she met Bill Clinton in 1971. Both were at this time law students at Yale. Along with his looks and easy charm, Bill was bright and idealistic – if not necessarily the most reflective of individuals. His disadvantaged background had given him insights into how ordinary people felt – along with a burning desire to get ahead. As a child in a violent household, he'd gained important survival skills – even if, inevitably, he'd suffered emotional damage too. Though he'd grown up in the segregationist South, he seems to have taken the Civil Rights message on board sincerely; he mixed unselfconsciously with African-Americans. The rigmarole surrounding his draft status, some might feel, showed signs of that genius for denial which was to become the hallmark of the man who much later said that, as a student at Oxford, he'd smoked marijuana but 'didn't inhale' and could solemnly

insist that he 'did not have sexual relations' with Monica Lewinsky. But in these exciting times such things weren't questioned and, since feminist consciousness hadn't as yet caught up with sexual liberation, his womanizing went unremarked (except by an enraged Hillary – though she still went ahead and married him in 1975).

In fairness, the importance of the 'Counterculture' in changing sexual behaviour is much exaggerated, certainly if we're to judge by anything in the history of the Presidency. It would be hard to find the hippie who used women more recklessly or ruthlessly than JFK or Lyndon Johnson. And, if Bill Clinton has the dubious honour of having been the first President to be sued for

Singing from the same hymn-sheet, Bill and Hillary Clinton are seen here in more innocent times, oblivious of troubles and controversies to come – but the bond between them has proved extraordinarily enduring.

sexual harassment, the appropriate legislation wouldn't have been in place before. But it's true that, for a variety of reasons – from unprecedented prosperity through the advent of the pill to the rejection of outdated gender roles – 'Baby Boomers' had an awful lot of fun.

Bill Beats the Draft

It's sometimes been suggested that America's young middle-class men dodged the call-up for Vietnam almost *en masse*, by getting themselves on to university or college courses or going on to grad school. This is all right as a rhetorical flight, but clearly overstates the case: many did enter the armed forces, whether willingly or reluctantly; a fair few openly defied the Draft.

Like many of his generation, Bill Clinton disapproved of the war and led demonstrations against it in America and England. During his time at Georgetown University, in 1967, he did an internship with J. William Fulbright, the anti-war Senator from Arkansas. But he never flat-out refused to serve. As a Georgetown student, he'd had exemption from the Draft, but his status changed when that course came to an end. The next academic year he spent largely in Oxford, England: he'd won a prestigious Rhodes Scholarship to study there. 'I am running away from something for the first time in my life,' he wrote to a friend.

In 1969, he applied and was admitted to Arkansas University's Reserve Officers' Training Corps (ROTC). In what some subsequently felt was a remarkably long

Boy of destiny, a young Bill Clinton comes face-to-face with his idol John F. Kennedy. Clinton was to take Kennedy as his model not just in political idealism but, as it turned out, in sexual conduct too.

Image- and presentation-wise the perfect politician, Bill Clinton most certainly looked the part as powerful US President, but his term of office was haunted by the 'character issue' from first to last.

and carefully worded letter, he wrote Colonel Eugene Holmes, the recruiter for Arkansas' ROTC, thanking him for his help in 'saving me from the Draft' and explaining his conscientious objections to the Vietnam War. Despite these objections, he said, he'd decided not to refuse, 'for one reason only, to maintain my political viability within the system'. Even at this early stage, he was determined (no doubt for the highest motives) to keep open the option of seeking public office.

Colonel Eugene Holmes later testified, in a notified letter, that he'd been told by the Draft Board that they were under 'pressure' from Fulbright's office to get Clinton into the ROTC. He denied having known – as Clinton's letter seemed to hint – that he'd been told of the applicant's work for the anti-war movement. If he'd known of this, he would surely have refused him as a recruit for the ROTC.

Clinton had in any case never turned up for his course at the University of Arkansas law school – choosing instead to go to Oxford and on to Yale – so he naturally hadn't been inducted into the ROTC there. In hindsight, Holmes concluded, that had never been his intention. He was convinced that the future-President had been playing for time – his formal enrolment for the ROTC in Arkansas had been enough to buy him a deferment from the Draft Board. In the event, when the lottery for the Draft had been held at the beginning of December 1969, Clinton's name had come out so far down the list that he was effectively exempt.

Rector's file came across his desk. There was no doubt that Ricky Ray had been a vicious criminal: having murdered a man in a night-club, he'd offered to turn himself in to a police officer, Robert Martin, then shot him callously down as he turned his back.

He'd then attempted suicide, but succeeded only in blowing away the frontal lobe of his own brain. The result was that he had the mentality of a toddler.

It was Hillary herself who in 1999 described her husband as 'a hard dog to keep on the porch' – an image surely more revealing that she meant.

Acting Tough

Through much of the 1980s, the politics of the Western world had been dominated by two great right-wingers. Ronald Reagan and Margaret Thatcher had been friends and fellow-radicals. Their popularity represented a real challenge to their political opponents: their rhetoric of individual freedom, personal responsibility and law and order had caught the imagination even of blue-collar workers and the lower-middle class. The parties of the Left had to find some way of making it clear that they were looking out for the respectable majority, and not afraid to slay a few sacred 'progressive cows'. British Prime Minister Tony Blair did it by backing the measures Margaret Thatcher had taken against the trade unions; Bill Clinton did it by sending a simple-minded black man to his death.

The Democrats had seen their candidate made mincemeat of by the Willie Horton ads of the George H.W. Bush campaign; Bill Clinton was resolved to exorcise that ghost. He found himself in a position to do just that, as Governor of Arkansas, when Ricky Ray

Seeing his chance to show he was unambiguously anti-crime, Clinton interrupted his campaign to come back and give the order for his execution. On 24 January 1992, Rector was led to the execution chamber to have a lethal injection administered. Notoriously, he left the dessert from his last meal, saying that he intended to come back and have it later.

Dogged by Scandal

It was Hillary herself who in 1999 described her husband as 'a hard dog to keep on the porch' – an image surely more revealing than she meant. Despite its folksy cheerfulness, it suggested a certain deep disdain, along with weary fatalism on the First Lady's part. It acknowledged the pointlessness of treating the leader of the Free World as an adult human, with all that meant in terms of moral responsibility.

Any politician has to be a persuader – and that's just a short step from a seducer, it might be said. Bill Clinton had an extraordinary talent for winning people

round – and an extraordinary need to do so. A psychologist might perhaps point to the fragility of an ego that, from childhood up, couldn't take love or acceptance completely for granted. The ease with which as a student he'd got the hard-bitten Senator Fulbright to take him on as his protégé – even the care he'd taken in schmoozing his Arkansas recruiter

Colonel Holmes before letting him down – suggested someone out of the usual run of opportunists.

But it was in his relations with women, of course, that Bill Clinton's drive to seduce was shown most spectacularly, and most damagingly. His first presidential campaign was almost derailed by the revelations of Gennifer Flowers. She claimed to have

WHITEWATER WHITEWASH?

BILL CLINTON'S VARIOUS SEX SCANDALS made for marvellous tabloid entertainment, but exasperated those commentators who felt that far more serious malfeasance wasn't receiving its due attention. Of less moment for them than the claim that Bill and Monica had made love in the Lincoln Bedroom of the White House was the revelation that – with the President's personal OK – this historic chamber had been rented out to campaign contributors for a total of $5.2 million. Questions were asked – but never effectively pursued – about Hillary's astonishing success in cattle futures trading: her $1000 investment had paid off a hundredfold. The First Couple were subpoenaed to give evidence after the collapse of the Whitewater Development Corporation, a Little Rock realty firm in which the Clintons had invested. In her capacity as lawyer, Hillary was alleged to have helped facilitate illegal deals. She thus became the first First Lady to be investigated for fraud. The prosecutors' failure to make their case might have exonerated her more resoundingly if so many

of her billing records from the relevant time hadn't been reported missing.

Whitewater, an evolving and apparently ever-growing scandal, became to conspiracy theorists what the Kennedy assassination had been, as unexplained deaths began to be added to the mix. White House Counsel Vince Foster was found dead of a gunshot wound in 1993; some questioned the official verdict of suicide.

Whitewater founder and Clinton friend Jim McDougal died in jail in 1998, after a mistake by his medical attendants. Secretary of Commerce Ron Brown and fundraisers C. Victor Raiser II and Hershell Friday were all killed in different plane crashes, thousands of miles apart ... Nothing untoward was ever found by the official investigations into these or other supposedly related fatalities, but for some the suspicion has never gone away.

Vince Foster was one of several Clinton aides and allies to die in mysterious circumstances: conspiracy theorists have worked hard to identify connections between these tragedies – though so far without success.

The friendly bear-hug Bill Clinton gives Monica Lewinsky here reveals no hint at all of their secret intimacies – all the controversy about cigars and semen-stains which was so soon to come to light.

had a 12-year affair with the then-Governor of Arkansas. Democrat supporters were quick to point to the apparent opportunism of the sometime *Penthouse*-model (who was subsequently to sell her story to that publication). To begin with, too, some of the details of that story were decidedly sketchy. The fact remained, though, that it all stacked up sufficiently to put the Presidential candidate in a difficult position. There were good reasons for doubting his denials – many took a 'no smoke without fire' view after years of gossip – and in 1998 Clinton actually made a partial admission of the affair.

Ironically (though somehow typically) his admission that he'd had sex with Gennifer Flowers came in the same deposition in which he 'emphatically' denied having tried to kiss and grope another woman, Kathleen Willey, while she'd been working in the White House Office in 1993. This in turn was being brought forward to defend the claim of *another* woman, Paula Jones, who'd worked in the Governor's Mansion in Little Rock, and who claimed to have been propositioned at that time. This case had first been brought in 1994 and had been working its way through the courts, Jones's lawyers strengthening their case along the way. Their aim was to build a body of evidence that the President of the United States was a serial sexual-harasser of women, and it has to be said that they didn't do too bad a job.

Monica's Moment

It was during the Paula Jones case that Clinton gave his first flat denial of having had an 'affair' with Monica Lewinsky. For what it's worth, the 22-year-old White House intern denied the claims as well – both Bill and Monica, it turned out, were sticklers for precision in the use of words. (As the weeks went on and the questions kept coming, ever more searching, the President was notoriously to voice doubts about exactly 'what the meaning of *is* is'.) Linda Tripp, a colleague in whom she'd confided – and who'd had the presence of mind (if that's what it was) to tape her confessions – tipped off Kenneth Starr, the Independent Counsel already investigating the President over other alleged irregularities.

Faced with perjury charges, Lewinsky offered to come clean in exchange for immunity from prosecution. Linda Tripp had persuaded her to keep Clinton's gifts – and not to dry-clean a dress which had been stained with semen and which now clinched the case against the President. As if this wasn't bad enough, Lewinsky testified that in one encounter Clinton had inserted a cigar into her vagina, giving

---

> Though the President strenuously denied any 'sexual relations' with Lewinsky and Hillary loyally blamed a right-wing conspiracy, he was found to have lied and held in contempt of court.

---

rise to innumerable ribald jokes. Though the President strenuously denied any 'sexual relations' with Lewinsky and Hillary loyally blamed a right-wing conspiracy, he was found to have lied and held in contempt of court.

Impeachment and Acquittal

The impeachment proceedings against Bill Clinton highlight the ineffectiveness of a system which is supposed to hold the Presidency to account, ensuring justice and impartiality in so doing. As with Andrew Johnson's case, however, moves against Bill Clinton quickly degenerated into an unseemly ruckus in which political partisanship appeared to have trumped any desire for justice. The impeachment, driven by Republican anger, was thwarted by Democratic loyalty: neither side could feel satisfaction at the outcome.

If Clinton's alleged crimes were squalid, some of that rubbed off on the proceedings against him. For

years, the air of Little Rock and Washington had been thick with rumours about the President's political and financial dealings, but he was now being arraigned about a semen-splash. When it came out that the President's most censorious critic, former Speaker Newt Gingrich, had actually embarked on an affair of his own in the course of the impeachment proceedings, any moral credibility the proceedings might have had was lost.

GEORGE W. BUSH, 2001–8

The defining event in George Walker Bush's childhood, it's been suggested, was the death of his younger sister Robin of leukaemia in 1953, when she was just three and he was only six. Prostrated by her loss, their mother Barbara is said to have become extra-protective in her treatment of all her children – particularly in the case of her eldest son. Hence, it's said, his helplessness; his inability to find his way in early adulthood; his lifelong reliance on the web of friends and contacts his father made. Yet this 'helplessness' (if that was ever really what it was) is as likely to be due to the overwhelming power of the paternal presence in his family. In the parade of Presidents George H.W. may cut a comparatively anonymous figure, but within his social milieu he seemed a titan. College friends of George W. recall that, while his contemporaries mocked and rebelled against their parents, he looked up to his father as though he were a god.

Claims that he was personally 'spoiled' or over-indulged are rejected by many who knew him at the time, but he obviously had a highly privileged upbringing. Despite his advantages, he struggled to match up: he found Andover, one of America's most prestigious prep schools, hard going and was well aware that he owed his admission to Yale not to his scintillating scholarly performance but to his status as a 'legacy' – an applicant whose father had been a graduate of the university. (That said, George W.'s much-vaunted 'stupidity' shouldn't be overstated: he was quick-witted and perceptive about people, friends

Born to rank and privilege he may have been, but George W. Bush had an unassuming and self-deprecating way about him which seemed to disarm opponents and also won over a sceptical electorate.

As times grew harder for America, George W. Bush's pampered background began to count against him more. Voters asked themselves how this preppy-president could really identify with what they were going through.

minded. He had a lot to be unassuming about, his critics might sneer, but the fact remains that unassuming is what he was. 'You never would have known who his father was, what kind of family he came from,' recalled Lanny Davis, a former fraternity brother who saw himself very much as George W.'s political foe.

It's good to be modest and to put people at their ease, of course, but it can also be extremely useful. It can be useful to be underestimated as well – and George W. had been underestimated all his life. He had a great gift, for one of his background and ambitions, of being free from any hint of patrician poise. It was to drive his opponents demented, the effortless way in which this most overprivileged of Yalies was able to get himself across as a pickup-driving good ol' boy.

from college days said, even if he never cut it as an academic. And that way of mangling the language which produced so many celebrated 'Bushisms' had been evident in the speech of his undoubtedly able father too.)

Perhaps it was the consciousness that he'd never meet his father's exacting standards; perhaps the winning charm he'd acquired in his relationship with his mom. Whatever the cause, George W. was much less arrogant than might be imagined – about either his abilities or his social class. Jokes about 'affirmative action' notwithstanding, indeed, George W. really was in a beleaguered minority at university: a legacy, a C-student among stars, and a dutiful conservative at a time when the cool campus radicals were massing on the Left. The Skull and Bones Club his father had joined had been an exclusive clique for the elite of the elite; now it was a sanctuary for the stuffy and out-of-touch. But George W. doesn't seem to have much

'Do Not Volunteer'

On graduating from Yale in 1968, George W. Bush became eligible for the Draft – at least in theory. Unlike Bill Clinton, he was proud to perform his patriotic duty, but he was able to do so without any risk of being sent anywhere near a combat zone. It had just been agreed at government level that the National Guard would not be required to go to Vietnam: suddenly, there was a clamour to get in. Ben Barnes, Lieutenant Governor of Texas at the time, testifies that, at the request of a mutual friend of his and George H.W., he made some calls and had young George moved up to the head of a 500-man waiting list. Serving alongside him in the Air National Guard for Texas were other sons of the elite: so much so that it was known as the 'Champagne Unit'. On signing up, applicants were invited – but not compelled – to put themselves forward for a tour of duty in Vietnam. George W. checked the box for 'do not volunteer'.

After two years, he was transferred to an Alabama base – at least in theory – though he didn't take his physicals or turn up for training: he was involved in a political campaign in Alabama, he told his squadron commander. Nominally, it seems he was transferred to an Alabama base, though there's no evidence he actually performed any service there, military or for that matter political. Journalist Dan Rather spoke to Jimmy and Linda Allison, old friends of George W.'s father who lived in Houston, and who recalled agreeing to keep an eye on young George on Dad's behalf. The 'Guardsman', said Linda, had spent his time 'raising a lot of hell in Houston … I had no idea that the National Guard was involved in his life in any way.'

Drugs and Drink

Precisely what 'a lot of hell' meant in George W.'s case was to be a matter of fierce debate during his Presidency. Bush family historian (and former Special Assistant to George H.W.) Bernard Lewis, got closer to the truth than most. George W. Bush gave him a series of interviews in the weeks leading up to his decision to run as President in 2000: these were recorded without his knowledge, and later leaked. The President-to-be was heard telling his interviewer that he wouldn't answer questions about his use of marijuana, ''cause I don't want some little kid doing what I tried'. He wanted to set a good example as President, he said. As for cocaine-use, this too got a 'non-denial denial': George W. didn't want to dignify these accusations with a response. It was time someone took a stand against the 'ugly' rumour-mongering he felt. He may also have felt, of course, that an explicit denial would be dangerous; that there might be so many potential witnesses 'out there'. Allegations of cocaine use at Yale and after had dogged him as he tried to take a tough line on drugs as Governor of Texas. Not surprisingly, they haven't gone away.

George W. Bush's problems with alcohol were well-attested: though he had stopped drinking back in 1986, there were persistent rumours that he had fallen off the wagon during his presidency.

Alcohol loomed even larger in George W.'s life, however. Drunken pranks were a feature of his student life, though his 1966 arrest for stealing a Christmas wreath off a hotel door hardly cuts it in a history of Presidential scandal. More serious was his conviction for driving under the influence a decade later. That his behaviour was a concern to his father (and might not be entirely unrelated to a certain resentment of the way the great man's presence dominated his life) seems to be confirmed by a widely reported stand-off between the two in 1972. After one drunk-driving incident in which George W. had driven over a garbage-can and perhaps endangered his younger brother Marvin, his father had given him a dressing-down, to which the young man had responded by challenging him to a *mano a mano* fight.

While never admitting to have been an 'alcoholic', George W. did say he'd quit drinking in 1986. Sources differ on how far his decision was linked to the influence of the evangelical preacher Billy Graham. There have been occasional claims of backsliding on the President's part, not least after the 'Pretzel Incident' of 2002. Bush briefly lost consciousness while watching a TV football game, fell off a sofa and injured his head. The official line was that, after feeling 'unwell' for a couple of days, he'd choked on a pretzel.

After the 2000 Florida poll, Americans learned far more than they'd ever wanted to about the technicalities of the voting process. To this day, Democrats believe this election was 'stolen' from them.

Others, then as previously, were sceptical – and yet it has to be said that, even if this and other claims were true, it could hardly be said that the President's life was being ruled by drink.

An Impostor in Power?

George W. Bush's Presidency was controversial from the off. The election had been 'stolen', his opponents said. Nationwide, the Democratic candidate Al Gore had garnered over half a million more votes than he, and there were accusations of irregularities in Florida in particular. There, a finely poised contest was finally ruled to have gone Bush's way with a majority of only 537 votes. Hundreds of ballots had been disqualified because – incompletely punched – they had 'dimpled', 'pregnant' or 'hanging' chads. Critics pointed as well to Bush's reliance on old friends of his father, most notably his Vice President Dick Cheney: George W. was a 'legacy' in the White House as he'd been before at Yale.

The event that was to dominate Bush's first term was the terrorist onslaught of 11 September 2001. His

LIKE FATHER, LIKE DAUGHTERS?

GEORGE W.'S DAUGHTERS, Barbara and Jenna, got into trouble in 2001 when they admitted using fake IDs to obtain alcohol under-age. Both girls had a reputation for partying hard, as their father had. Reports that the twins smoked marijuana (in one alleged incident of 2003, with the actor Ashton Kutcher) were never proved. Whether because they'd settled down and started behaving better or simply acquired a bit more discretion, they managed for the most part to keep themselves out of the news thereafter.

Jenna Bush fell foul of the Texas authorities when she was caught in possession of alcohol under-age in April 2001. Twin sister Barbara was arrested on similar charges just a few weeks later.

response 'made' his Presidency, though it very nearly broke it. Reading a story-book, *The Pet Goat*, to children in a Florida elementary school when news of the attacks came in, he carried on reading for several minutes. 'Indecisive', said his enemies; 'calm under fire', said his friends. Reactions divided pretty much along party lines. The same was true for his declaration of a 'War on Terror' in the days that followed and, more specifically, his invasion of Iraq. Though they'd strongly hinted at a link between former-US ally Saddam Hussein and the Al Qaeda attacks of 9/11, no real evidence for this (inherently improbable) connection was ever forthcoming. Neither, even after the conquest of Iraq, was there ever any sign of the weapons of mass-destruction Bush and his supporters had maintained that the dictator had been ready to deploy. More seriously, some felt, the ideal of liberty was becoming as elusive as any weapons-lab, with a Patriot Act at home and rumours of rendition for torture overseas.

Heroes and Villains

The Democrats had high hopes for their candidate in the Presidential Elections of 2004: John Kerry was something of a secret weapon. A Vietnam veteran who'd been decorated for valour, he seemed just the man to get the message across for a party so often sneered at as 'peaceniks' by the Right. While the President had sat out the War in the United States, serving (when he felt like it) with the Air National Guard in Texas, Kerry had been out there risking his life for his country. This was notable given the accusations that George W. Bush had lacked decision in the immediate aftermath of the 9/11 terrorist attacks. By this time too, the President had given his notorious 'Mission Accomplished' speech aboard the USS *Abraham Lincoln* – and it was clear that America's work in Iraq was actually anything but done. One way and another, then, it looked as though Bush was vulnerable where all things military were concerned. John Kerry could take him on in this area and win.

It didn't work out that way. Instead, a synthetic 'controversy' blew up over the courageous actions

Muslim prisoners were held at Guantánamo Bay for years after their capture in Afghanistan and elsewhere. Allegations of torture flew, and few inmates were ever to be tried – or even to face coherent charges.

Iraqi journalist Muntadar al-Zaidi expressed the contempt of many in the Arab world for George W. Bush, when he stood up and hurled his shoes at the bemused President at a press conference in 2008.

which had won the swift boat commander his Silver Star. Whilst his former crewmates all agreed on his heroism, a group of veterans with connections to the Bush campaign took out ads claiming to have discredited the Democratic candidate. And people believed it – enough people, at least, to help swing things Bush's way.

A Reputation in Recession

When the devastatingly powerful Hurricane Katrina hit New Orleans in 2005, Washington's response was slow and uncoordinated: the President had failed miserably to show any real leadership, it was said. To add flames to the fire, it didn't help that so many of the victims were poor and black: the now-traditional suspicion that the Republicans were unsympathetic to the poor and tolerant of racism found a dramatic focus. Yet, while critics railed against the 'moral bankruptcy' of George W.'s Presidency, it was actual, non-figurative financial ruin that sealed its failure politically. Already accused of dropping the ball over Katrina, the President was caught out badly two years later when financial crisis dragged the United States into a deep recession. The President got it both ways: on the one hand his attempts to restore economic stability were deemed woefully tardy and inadequate; on the other, there was outrage that he was apparently showing so much more concern for middle-class investors (and, worse still, wealthy bankers) than he had for the poor people of New Orleans.

Bush's Republicans were left in an impossible position. John McCain fought a doughty campaign, whilst Sarah Palin's sudden arrival from Alaska transformed the landscape on the political right. Yet, colourful and controversial as she was, she couldn't contend with the wave of optimism and idealism which by now was sweeping the first ever African-American President White House-ward. How far Barack Obama would fulfil the hopes invested in him, how well he would acquit himself in the office of President, were questions for which there could as yet be no answer.

A LOYAL LITTLE BROTHER

JOHN 'JEB' BUSH APPEARED TO BE everything his elder brother wasn't: he finished his University of Texas degree (in Latin American Studies) with impressive grades. Limiting his 'acting out' to marrying a Mexican girl – a masterstroke, as it turned out, for a Florida politician – he followed in his father's footsteps with both conscientiousness and flair. He secured the Governorship of Florida, the second attempt, in 1998.

Florida was one of the key states in the 'stolen' election of 2000, though how far any wrongdoing can be laid at Jeb's door is debatable. Alleged polling malpractices apart, police checkpoints were said to have been set up to intimidate black voters (presumed to be Democrats) in Florida's cities. But these claims weren't proven – and besides, Jeb was hardly the only important Republican in the state. That he supported the Bush campaign was to be expected – after all, he

was a Bush; the Presidential candidate was his brother and a fellow-Republican.

In 2006 George H.W. broke down and sobbed as he addressed a Tallahassee conference, recalling the courage Jeb had shown in adversity when – unjustly, he implied – he'd lost the race for Florida State Governor in 1994. 'He didn't whine about it. He didn't complain …' Opponents of George W. were quick to decide that he had been drawing an implicit contrast with the character of the son then occupying the White House, though in truth the evidence for this conclusion was never clear.

The President who might have been (and might yet be?), 'Jeb' Bush showed more obvious promise than his elder brother: it's been suggested that George H.W. Bush regarded him as his true heir.

PICTURE CREDITS